Cherokee
Little People

Yuñwi Tsunsdi'

The Secrets and Mysteries of the

Cherokee
Little People

Yuñwi Tsunsdi'

Written and Illustrated
by
Lynn King Lossiah

Art on Title Pages by Ernie Lossiah

Cherokee Publications

Cherokee , North Carolina

Cherokee Publications, Cherokee, NC 28719
Copyrighted © 1998 by Lynn King Lossiah

Third Edition
Printed in the United States of America

ISBN 0-935741-22-4
       978-0-935741-22-3

Text & Illustrations by Lynn King Lossiah
Title pages illustrated by Ernie Lossiah

First Printing - 1998
Second Printing - 2002
Third Printing (Language Edition) - 2008

THIS BOOK IS DEDICATED TO:

Lillian Shell Lossiah

(Ernie's mother)
for being

"MOM"

A Very Special Thanks to

Shannon Swimmer and Family
Gilliam Jackson
and
The Cherokee Immersion Students and Instructors

For the Cherokee Language Translation

Forward

Here is your opportunity to share in Cherokee life and experience, to gain a glimpse into a part of their world clothed in secret and mystery, to appreciate with them the "Yuñwi Tsunsdi'," the Little People who have coexisted with them for untold centuries.

There are countless stories and encounters out of which these few are selected to give some understanding of who the Little People are and what part they play in the lives of the Cherokee people, their trials and tragedies, fun and laughter, morals and teachings, mysteries and secrets as never told before.

No need to analyze and fictionalize this material or try to categorize it with myths, fables and legends. It is simply available here for those who wish to listen and to interpret within their own personal freedom. So, whether you are prone to deny the validity of this material as fact, or ready to stretch your mind to areas of our environment previously unknown to you, or find yourself comparing these to similar unexplained experiences of your own, relax, be open to mystery and allow for phenomena of nature beyond your present experience.

One thing is sure, those who venture into these pages will find an enjoyment beyond the usual and will not close the book without having learned more about themselves which they will, undoubtedly, want to share with others.

This is only a beginning, a bare tapping of the source of material available on this subject. The author welcomes further inquiry from those who wish to pursue more information on the Little People, the "Yuñwi Tsunsdi'" of the Cherokee.

Contents

Introduction - note from the author

This book is derived from a large body of material collected from the Cherokee people and written sources including James Mooney, noted authority of Cherokee history and mythology. Personal reports have been rewritten into story form for the reader without the loss or the alteration of essential information and events.

The book starts with "The Oldest Story Ever Told" of a particular "Little People Who Wore White." The content of this story may suggest infiltration of Biblical inclinations into Cherokee culture and legendry. However, as one reads closely and remembers the approximate time of the birth of the story, it appears to date before this knowledge was available to the Cherokee. This story was passed through the family of Goingback (G.B.) Chiltoskey, written down by his wife, Mary Ulmer Chiltoskey, two of Cherokee's most treasured and trusted people.

The reports following this story are from *Myths and Sacred Formulas of the Cherokees* written by James Mooney from the Nineteenth and Seventeenth annual ethnology reports to Congress for the Smithsonian around 1900. Mooney included in his research information dating back to 1557 gained through his time spent living among the Cherokee from 1887 to 1890.

The remaining events with the Little People are taken from Mooney's time to the present day, reported by people of the Eastern Band of Cherokees living on the Qualla Boundaries (reservations) in western North Carolina within the Great Smoky Mountains, the land of a thousand smokes.

The purpose of the book is to introduce to the reader a vital part of the Cherokee culture as it has never before been presented, the secrets and mysteries of the Cherokee Little People.

NOTE:

Archaeologist and technology have brought to truth some of the Cherokee myths and legends. Those who denounce the existence of the Little People are referred to the desecrated burial sites where skeletons of adults less than three feet tall have been found buried both singularly and with normal height adults. This technology has recorded dates of such sites through centuries on Native American land as well as spots all over the planet.

From a time beyond memory to present day the Little People, in their death, have outlived the "superstition" stigma.

THE OLDEST STORY EVER TOLD

The Cherokee, **Tsa-la-gi**, used to greet the morning sun in prayer each day. They had gathering places near their villages along the winding courses of the rivers and streams or by the waterfalls. They would go into the water, immersing themselves to cleanse their bodies, minds, and spirit. This ritual was done daily, in all seasons, to keep them in touch with truth and purpose.

One of their gathering places was the area now covered by the water of Fontana Lake in North Carolina not far from Cherokee Qualla, **Tsa-la-gi Qua-li**, Boundaries. It was then known as Judson. From this area comes the *Oldest Story Ever Told*.

It is reported that the native people of Turtle Island (North America) knew what was happening all over the world. They talked about small people-like creatures covered with hair who traveled through the trees (monkeys), horses with necks longer than their bodies (giraffe), or the ones that were striped black and white (zebras) and many more animals that did not inhabit the land of Turtle Island.

They knew about other lands and other peoples. Some even sent friendly messages back and forth. They shared ideas with these people from the other side of the ocean.

There seems to be evidence that many people all over the planet knew that the earth was round before science and adventurers proved it. Some Native Americans were skilled as astronomers, medalists, chemists, architects and other trades. They knew of other mountain ranges, of the pyramids, of markings on giant cliffs, of other seas, places of power, and many wonders of the world. For the Native Americans, this knowledge was possible because of the *LITTLE-PEOPLE-WHO-WORE-WHITE.*

According to **Tsa-la-gi** tradition these special Little People, **Yuñwi Tsunsdi'**, travelled all over the world and brought back news to Turtle Island.

The Oldest Story Ever Told

The eastern sky brightened, turning pink with morning. The prayers were completed and everyone was in greetings. Someone called attention to beautiful lights coming toward them in a distance. A gust of wind swept through the forest preceding the hoot of an owl, **u-gu-gu**, over the river.   They stood awe-struck as the Little-People-Who-Wore-White took form from the lights.

When the Little-People-Who-Wore-White arrived, sadness surrounded them in such a way that they did not talk. They kept their heads down in sorrow and stayed to themselves. Soon the gathering could feel all of nature being affected by this sadness. The Cherokees, **Tsa-la-gi**, did not have much to say to one another.

There was an old Cherokee, **Tsa-la-gi**, man who had been meeting the Little-People-Who-Wore-White longer than anyone else present. He made his way where they were and waited to be noticed. One of the Little-People-Who-Wore-White left the others and took the old man into the woods. They were gone for some time.

When they returned, the old man began speaking to the crowd. He reminded them of a time about 33 years before. It was the same time the new star came in the east, and a special child was born across the ocean. He reviewed all the news they had heard of him, from time to time, while he was growing up. How this special boy had become a man and had taught a better way to live. He reminded the gathering of this man's visits, through spirit, to tribes of this land.

The old man had returned the smiles to the **Tsa-la-gi** by talking about this man they had grown to love but had not seen.

The Little-People-Who-Wore-White joined the old man and spoke, "This man who brought you the knowledge of the way of peace and harmony among yourselves and all things, this man who everyone loves if they are willing to hear him, has enemies. The enemies refuse to hear his message. They refuse to see when he works the miracles before their own eyes. These enemies who love only their positions and pursuit of material wealth have conspired against him. Today, when the sky darkens they will have killed him in a strange and most horrible way."

The **Tsa-la-gi** began to sing to this special man of peace as they watched the skies. They sang until the day became as dark as night. The nearby creatures of the woods came among them and shared the sorrow. All of nature grieved.

The next day the Little-People-Who-Wore-White were still among those gathered. When the **Tsa-la-gi** were leaving to go back to their own villages they were told, "No one, if not the Great Spirit, could stop this tragic thing that has happened. Take what new teachings you have learned from Him and live them in His honor."

The **Tsa-la-gi** managed to make their way home but could not manage their tears. Through the blur a woman saw tiny crystal-like sparkles on the trail. She reached down and picked one up. She showed it to her friend. Soon everyone had picked one up.

The people observed that wherever a tear fell on these little stones it formed a tiny cross. It was a gift and a sign from the Great Spirit who heard their compassion and showed his love for them. These crosses of stone were kept and cherished by the **Tsa-la-gi**, and until this day are found and treasured by many.

About 2000 years have passed since then, but that day is still remembered among the **Tsa-la-gi** through these tiny crosses of stone.

However, for the last two centuries destruction of beautiful land areas has been rampant. What was sacred to the **Tsa-la-gi** has now been desecrated. The tiny stone crosses have been covered with dammed up water, plowed over, bulldozed and covered with concrete. Many of the **Tsa-la-gi** still know the power of these stones, but they are harder to find now. Others do not understand, and apparently, the stones are only a novelty to them.

13

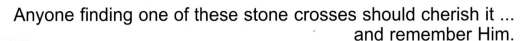

Anyone finding one of these stone crosses should cherish it ... and remember Him.

Today these stones are sparsely found in other **Tsa-la-gi** meeting places, what are now commonly called Fairyland Park in Virginia and Tallulah Falls in Georgia.

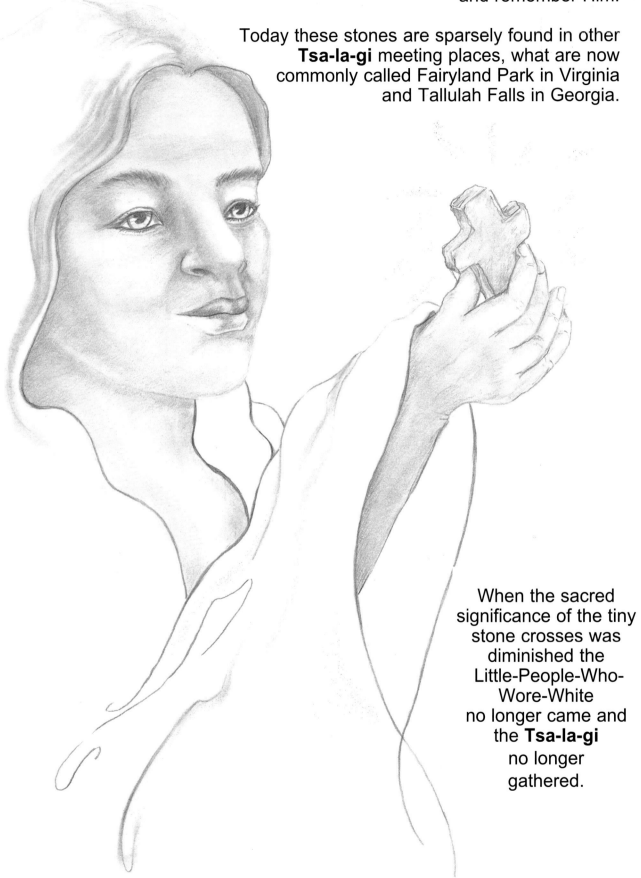

When the sacred significance of the tiny stone crosses was diminished the Little-People-Who-Wore-White no longer came and the **Tsa-la-gi** no longer gathered.

RECORDED HISTORY
OF THE
LITTLE PEOPLE

as told in

Mooney's Myths and Sacred Formulas
of the Cherokee

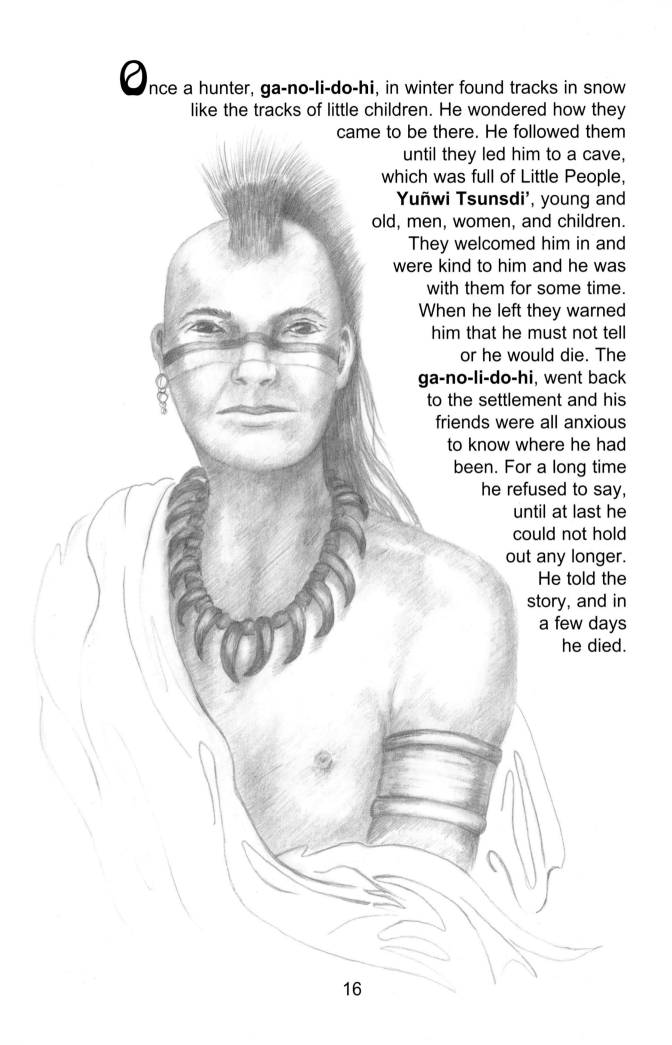

Once a hunter, **ga-no-li-do-hi**, in winter found tracks in snow like the tracks of little children. He wondered how they came to be there. He followed them until they led him to a cave, which was full of Little People, **Yuñwi Tsunsdi'**, young and old, men, women, and children. They welcomed him in and were kind to him and he was with them for some time. When he left they warned him that he must not tell or he would die. The **ga-no-li-do-hi**, went back to the settlement and his friends were all anxious to know where he had been. For a long time he refused to say, until at last he could not hold out any longer. He told the story, and in a few days he died.

16

Two hunters, **a-ni-ga-no-li-do-hi**, from Raventown, while going behind the high fall near the head of Oconaluftee river on the Eastern Cherokee reservation, found a cave there with fresh foot prints of the Little People, **Yûñ´wi Tsunsdi´** all over the floor.

When a hunter, **ga-no-li-do-hi**, finds anything in the woods, such as a knife or a trinket, he must say "Little People, I want to take this," "**Yûñ´wi Tsunsdi´, Ha-tlv go-hwe**", because it may belong to them, and if he does not ask permission they will throw stones at him as he goes home.

17

During the smallpox among the East Cherokee, just after the Civil War, one sick man wandered off. His friends searched but could not find him. After several weeks he came back and said that the Little People, **Yûñ´wi Tsunsdi'**, had found him and taken him to one of their caves and tended to him until he was cured.

man named Tsantawu' was lost in the mountains. It was winter time and very cold. He was gone for a long time. Two weeks had passed. After sixteen days he came back. He told that the Little People, **Yûñ´wi Tsunsdi´**, had found him and taken him to their cave. There he had been well treated, and given plenty of everything to eat except bread. He wanted the bread and took some anyways.

They were large loaves, but when he took them into his hand to eat they seemed to shrink into small cakes so light and crumbly that though he might eat all day he would not be satisfied. Tsantawu' did not take anymore of their bread.

After he was well rested they walked him part of the way home. They came to a small creek, about knee-deep, where they told him to wade across to reach the main trail on the other side.

He waded across and turned to look back, but the **Yûñ´wi Tsunsdi´**, were gone and the creek was a deep river. When he reached home his legs were frozen to the knees and he lived only a few days. Did Tsantawu' die because he stole bread from the **Yûñ´wi Tsunsdi´**?

19

Looking back
into the yesterdays,
rewards,
regrets,
but always
a learning to apply
today....for tomorrow.

Sometimes, the Little People, **Yûñ´wi Tsundi´**,
would come near a house at night and the people
inside would hear them talking, but they
would not go out, and in the morning
they would find the corn, **se-lu**,
gathered or the field cleared
as if a whole force of
men had been at work.

*Always remember —
do not watch.*

Once the Little People,
Yûñ´wi Tsunsdi´, had been very kind
to the people of a certain settlement, helping
them at night with their work and taking good care of
any lost children, until something happened to offend them and
they made up their minds to leave
the neighborhood.

Those who were watching at the time saw the whole company of
Yûñ´wi Tsunsdi´, come down to a ford in the river and cross over and
disappear into the mouth of a large cave on the other side. They were never
heard of near the settlement again.

How The Kingfisher Got His Bill

A blacksnake, **gu-le-gi**, found a Yellowhammer's nest in a hollow tree. After swallowing the young birds, he coiled up to sleep in the nest. The mother found him when she came back. She went for help to the Little People, **Yûñ´wi Tsunsdi´**, who sent her to the Kingfisher.

Kingfisher came to her nest. After flying back and forth past the hole a few times, he made one dart at the snake and pulled him out dead. When they looked they found a hole in the snake's head where the Kingfisher had pierced it with a slender **tugãlû´nå** fish, which he carried in her bill like a lance.

From this, the Little People, **Yûñ´wi Tsunsdi´**, concluded that Kingfisher would make a first class gigger if he only had the right spear, so they gave him his long bill as a reward.

Every now and then, a child with special qualities is born. Such a child is known by signs and wonders on the earth or in the skies. Such signs are thought to indicate a leader, prophet or person of Spiritual gifts. The birth of twins with such signs accompanying are thought to have very special significance.

In ancient times, these newborns were kept in seclusion for their first day of life, tended only by their mother and fed only the juice of corn hominy. For their first two years, they were given free reign to do anything they wanted without discipline. As they grew older, they were encouraged to go out alone in the forests and talk with the Little People.

These children grew up to be prophets and Spiritual leaders.

WHO
ARE
THE
LITTLE
PEOPLE

The first missionaries who came to live with the Cherokees, **Tsa-la-gi** were good people. Many of them were very narrow in their views, however, and branded those outside their own beliefs as pagans of superstition and denounced their beliefs. The Little People, **Yûñ´wi Tsunsdi´**, were marked as mere fable and falsehood. In the mind of the **Tsa-la-gi**, a logical person must either deny all miracles and mysteries of nature or none of them, and one must have reason for disbelief.

The **Tsa-la-gi** people did not readily discuss the **Yûñ´wi Tsunsdi´** with the missionaries. They were not interested in debating the issue. When they did share information with them it was to help the missionaries to know how to live with the **Yûñ´wi Tsunsdi´** in respect and enjoy the help they gave.

Today, the **Yûñ´wi Tsunsdi´** may seem fewer in numbers, or do not appear as readily, but observation tells us that the proof of the **Yûñ´wi Tsunsdi´** existence is independent of the critics' opinion or spiritual arrogance.

The elders say that when the Northern Europeans first came and lived in peace with the **Tsa-la-gi**, the **Yûñ´wi Tsunsdi´** were obvious and helped them also.

Jt is not easy to see the Little People, **Yûñ´wi Tsunsdi´**, in broad daylight. They often hide from mortal eyes by appearing in the sun's brightness. The **Yûñ´wi Tsunsdi´** can see through the brightness.

The **Yûñ´wi Tsunsdi´** cannot be seen at night unless there is a bright moon. Their light has been seen in the forest at night, however, close to the ground, moving through the trees, just off the trails. One can only catch up with their lights if the **Yûñ´wi Tsunsdi´** want them to.

The **Yûñ´wi Tsunsdi´** are most often seen at dusk or dawn. They like to be with the animals when they feed, gathering the plants with the deer, **a-wi**, fishing with the bears, **yo-na**, picking up their firewood with the beaver, **do-yi**, or visiting the native people, escorted by the fox, **tsu-la**.

They have co-existed with the Cherokee, **Tsa-la-gi**, people for countless centuries and look like full bloods, dark skinned, black eyes, and with straight black hair that reaches to the ground. They are handsome and strong and no more than three feet tall.

They have always dressed as the **Tsa-la-gi** people dress at any given time of their history.

They speak in an ancient **Tsa-la-gi** dialect. Some of the elders today can understand this strange dialect and know what they are saying. Some say it is Elati, a **Tsa-la-gi** language now extinct.

They have their own communties or clans throughout the mountains. Like the **Tsa-la-gi**, each community has its own jokers and serious people, leaders and followers, trouble makers and thinkers, dreamers, doctors, hunters and gatherers.

Communication

Walk into the forest and listen. Discover the musical voice of the stream as it plays its melody over rocks and boulders strewn in its path. Rest on the soft green-covered welcome mat by the stream. Examine the innocent beauty that surrounds you, the towering oaks that moan age old secrets to each other through the wind, composing hushing sounds as it moves through the groves of jackpine. Feel the sun dancing through the hardwoods, teasing you with its warmth. Hear the tales of mystical journeys shared by all of nature around you. You are in the home of the Little People and are experiencing the sounds and sights of their habitation.

Nature is a world of its own, civilizations of winged ones, crawling colonies, the travelers of the finned, and the four-legged communities.

Nature holds the long guarded secrets, the truths of universal existence, individualized yet compatible reality. Should you journey into that unique reality, with an inner sense of hearing the special language of it, you could comprehend the finiteness of each of its species of people. Then, perhaps you will see and know the fascinating history of the centuries old trees, the millennium aged rocks, the ancient formations of streams and waterfalls, and realize that here are the Little People, comfortable among the mystifying enigmas of the ages.

We, the two-legged species remain alienated from all of this unless we take the time to go walking into the forest, the habitat of the Little People, and listen.

Rock Cave Clan

NV-U-SDA-GI-LV TSU-NI-YV-WI

The rock, **nv-ya**, caves on the mountain sides are the preferred homes of the Rock Cave Little People, **Yûñ´wi Tsunsdi'**. They like to help the native people. They do chores for them when they get behind, bring them medicine plants when they are sick, watch after their children when they are busy.

Just like the Cherokees, **Tsa-la-gi,** they have been pushed into smaller areas to live. They make themselves less visible because of the constant invasion.

Sometimes the **Yûñ´wi Tsunsdi´** are mischievous, but they are only playing tricks on people to remind them how others should be treated. Their message is: "How one treats others is how he will be treated and remember whatever you do, you will eventually experience that which is similar." It is important for them to help humans maintain balance and harmony, the cause and effect of living.

31

Tree Clan

TSU-GA-I TSU-NI-YV-WI

Some communities of the Little People, **Yûñ´wi Tsunsdi´**, live among the trees. The old trees like their company and feel more useful when playing host to them. Their huge trunks with hollow passageways provide good housing, and their large roots act as private entrances. They drop their old limbs to warn the Little People, **Yûñ´wi Tsunsdi´**, when someone is approaching.

These **Yûñ´wi Tsunsdi´** like to help their nature friends, the winged and four-legged and the crawling ones. The snakes are their companions and together they provide protection for all the others.

They, are known as being mischievous, but they are only letting humans know when there is a lack of respect for nature such as failure to respect the homes of others, especially out of carelessness or when it is due to a quest for personal gain.

They may cause things to happen to you and have things taken away from you so you will remember: Mother earth provides all we need for shelter, food, and clothing if we do not take too much or use it wrongly. When man takes too much for himself, kills needlessly or denies nature's right for life, it leaves others without.

32

Laurel Clan

TSU-GA- I TSU-NI-YV-WI

The community of the Little People, **Yûñ´wi Tsunsdi´**, who live among the laurels like to help with plant nourishing. Wherever there is a need or problem, they are ready to help. Whether it is a large cornfield that provides for an entire tribe or a small garden, they love to nourish the land and plants insuring good crops. If an area has been burned out, flooded or hit by a drought they nourish any plants surviving and help them to recover at that same place if possible. If not, they move plants to different areas to grow. Nothing becomes extinct with the help of these little people.

The **Yûñ´wi Tsunsdi´** of this group are not encountered very much anymore. As the laurel has been cut away, they go further and further into the undisturbed mountains. They still come to help when the plants are challenged, but the job becomes very difficult as man keeps adding to nature's destruction. They try to discourage man from his own devastation by planting certain warrior plants around everything that he builds when respect for plant life and its value is ignored.

The Laurel **Yûñ´wi Tsundi´** teach us not to take our "perceived" needs too seriously. They encourage us to be happy with what is provided and share with others. People who do this will have healthy plants, gardens and orchards, and they will always have plenty.

Dogwood Clan

KN-NV-SI-TI   TSU-NI-YV-WI

A special group of Little People, **Yûñ´wi Tsunsdi´**, live among the dogwood, **kv-nv-si-ti**, trees. These people are very delicate, both physically and emotionally. They look for only the good and beauty in everyone and in all things. They can be seen only when they choose to reveal themselves with the dogwood blossoms, **kn-nv-si-ti u-tsi-lo-hv.**

They spend the rest of their time "dreaming" of good things for all people, animals, plants, those who swim, those who crawl and those who fly. They care for everything that mother earth provides.

When they do appear and look around, their tears become the **kn-nv-si-ti u-tsi-lo-hv.** Some seasons the tears are scant and fall quickly, other seasons the petals linger and are full. It depends on whether humans are treating each other and all things with consideration, especially our mother earth.

They are never known to be mischievous. All year they dream of helping each other from sincere and caring hearts, rather than for personal gain.

34

Thunderbeings

ANI'-HYUN' TIK WA-LA'SKI

According to legend, it took thousands of cycles for the Thunderbeings, **Ani'-hyun' tik wa-la'ski**, wings to mature. Before that, **Ani'-hyun' tik wa-la'ski** lived in the cocoons of the clouds, **u-lo-gi-lv**, and fed upon the rains, **a-ga-sga**. Some versions of the story say that **Ani'-hyun' tik wa-la'ski** could become human beings if they chose to. They could send their spirits down to earth in the form of bolts of lightening, **a-na-ga-li-s-k(i)**; when the bolt struck near a woman's womb, the spirit could go inside and grow into a human. They would, however, only grow to maybe three feet tall when an adult. To the Cherokee, **Tsa-la-gi**, they are called "The Thunderers." They bring great power and wisdom to the people of the earth.

It is said they do not come as much in these days because the race of destroyers has infested our mother earth, global-wide. The earth people have become weak from fighting this mind-disease. In this era it is time for the **Ani'-hyun' tik wa-la'ski** to use their power and wisdom only from the **u-lo-gi-lv**, the wind, **u-no-le**, and **a-ga-sga**, creating more frequent damaging floods, extreme droughts, and uncommonly forceful winds. Their power and wisdom is used now to protect mother earth rather than the human beings who inhabit her.

35

With myths and legends,
one cannot be sure,
for it is often disguised
until
time reveals
its reasoning.

All things are real,
yet
there is so much reality
we do not know.

Today,
what we rely on
as truth
will be disguised
in the tomorrows.

Only myths and legends
appear again.

The Most Frequent Stories Told

The stories on the following pages are taken from actual reports of encounters with the Little People, **Yûñ´wi Tsunsdi´**

Many Cherokee, **Tsa-la-gi**, people talk about having seen or heard the **Yûñ´wi Tsunsdi´**. More than a few have the same story.

These stories are the most frequently told and are compiled from reports given by , members of the Eastern Band of Cherokee Indians, **A-ni-tsa-la-gi'**, in Western North Carolina. The reports date from the later nineteenth century to the present time.

When the Little People, **Yûñ´wi Tsunsdi´**, visit Cherokee, **Tsa-la-gi**, homes, the kitchen seems to be their favorite room of the house. They like bright things such as silverware, pots and pans or shiny appliances. According to many stories, one can often hear these items being moved around and afterward find them out of place. They seem to come to play with these things or to look at themselves in the mirror surfaces. They don't usually take anything unless they are hungry.

Since the Little People, **Yûñ´wi Tsunsdi´**, seem to especially enjoy it, the Cherokee, **Tsa-la-gi**, women often leave cornbread, **se-lu ga-du**, for them on the kitchen table. Frequently, the women report, the **se-lu ga-du** is gone the next day with crumbs left on the table or trailing across the room to the kitchen door. Some have heard the kitchen door closing, knowing that the **Yûñ´wi Tsunsdi´** had gotten their fill of **se-lu ga-du** and left.

39

Many share stories of hearing chairs scoot across the kitchen floor and cabinets opening and closing as if the **Yûñ´wi Tsunsdi´** were looking for something.

A few have seen them in bedrooms, but they are more often spotted in hallways like "shadows on the edge of your vision." Muffled footsteps or whispers, like that of children at play, sometimes accompany the shadows.

When the **Yûñ´wi Tsunsdi´** come and go they can be heard crossing the porch, walking in carports or near the backdoor. The sounds are soft like children at play wearing moccasins.

Many stories are told of missing items, gone one minute and reappearing somewhere else the next. Some **Yûñ´wi Tsunsdi´** like to tease, and things don't reappear for some time. In some cases, they are never found. "Perhaps they forget," suggested one elder woman.

A lot of the older **Tsa-la-gi** are helped by the **Yûñ´wi Tsunsdi´** in finding things such as eyeglasses. Often they just ask them for help, and the items reappear nearby on the table or by their favorite chair. Lost garden tools are often returned by the **Yûñ´wi Tsunsdi´** when asked.

Equally frequent are the stories of children being lost in the mountains. Often they were thought of as having been "taken" by the **Yûñ´wi Tsunsdi´** and later "brought home" by them.

They Want
You To
Believe
In Them

If you do things deliberately
to prove you do not believe in them,
like disturb where they might live,
or mock their singing and drumming,
or even dispute someone who does believe in them,
the Little People will help you to believe.

On a clear moon-lit night two men, **ta-li a-sga-ya**, were walking down a dirt road. A hard day of work had tired them and they did not relish the long walk home. As they were passing a cornfield, **tso-ge-di**, one said, "You know, if we cut through the field, we'll get home a lot quicker."

"Well what are we waiting for?" his friend replied, and they both turned into the field, each following a row of corn, **se-lu**, with a few rows between them. The road disappeared behind tall stalks of **se-lu** as sharp green leaves sliced at their faces and rubbed at their shirt sleeves.

The **ta-li a-sag-ya** had not walked long before they heard the rustle of **se-lu** ahead. They heard the sound of scuffling and quiet laughter, growing louder as it drew closer. Suddenly, out of the darkness between the rows of **se-lu** a party of Little People, **Yûñ´wi Tsunsdi´**, tromped right through the midst of the **ta-li a-sag-ya**, leaving them speechless. Thirteen in all, they marched noisily along, one or two poking their heads through the stalks to glance curiously at the men, **a-sga-ya**, but otherwise paying them little attention.

The **ta-li a-sag-ya** knew it was a band of the **Yûñ´wi Tsunsdi´** that they saw. Many wondered about this since it is believed that the **Yûñ´wi Tsunsdi´** show themselves only to the Cherokee, **Tsa-la-gi**, and one of the **a-sga-ya** was white. Whatever the case, the men watched as the little group left the **tso-ge-sdi**, crossed the dirt road and vanished into the darkness near a mountainside.

43

A stranger, **ka-lo-i**, once came to Cherokee, **Tsa-la-gi**, during the hunting season. He wore a red bandanna under his beat-up old hat and had a scruffy black beard that was always itching him. He fancied himself an adventurer and loved to brag about his latest kill, bouncing up and down on the heels of his boots to emphasize the dangerous points.

44

Most people listened with a raised eyebrow as he would work himself up to a crescendo and then jump in his pickup and drive off in search of game again.

45

One day, his search led him far into the hills where paved highways ended and dusty mountain roads snaked their way into the mountain coves. He drove until dusk and set up camp near the foot of a tall cliff that glowed white from the evening sun.

After a meager meal of cold beans and bread he grew restless. He wanted to hunt, but it was getting too dark. To satisfy himself, he loaded his rifle and started shooting randomly into the forest, aiming at the limbs and leaves and anything else that presented itself. He became especially attracted to shooting into the white cliff side.

"What are you doing?" asked an old man, **u-ta-so-nv-hi**, who appeared without warning. "Practicing," replied the hunter, **ga-no-li-do-hi**, taking a bead on a particularly round stone in the cliff.

"Do you not care that people live nearby and might be sleeping?"

"No people around here as I can see. Where did you come from anyway?" asked the **ga-no-li-do-hi**, with a grin.

The **u-ta-so-nv-hi** nodded toward a nearly concealed log cabin. A dim light in the window was the only noticeable evidence that a cabin was there.

The **ga-no-li-do-hi** glanced unconcerned in that direction then took a few more shots as the **u-ta-so-nv-hi** stood silently watching. The **ga-no-li-do-hi** had almost forgotten that he was there when the **u-ta-so-nv-hi** spoke again, "You're disturbing the Little People, **Yûñ´wi Tsunsdi´**."

The **ga-no-li-do-hi** looked at the **u-ta-so-nv-hi** and frowned. "The little what?"

"The **Yûñ´wi Tsunsdi´**," the **u-ta-so-nv-hi** repeated and pointed upward to the cliff. "They live around the cliff where you are shooting. It won't be good for you if you anger them."

It took a moment for the **ga-no-li-do-hi** to comprehend. Then he laughed out loud and said, "I don't believe in such tales, old man." He continued to shoot and nothing the **u-ta-so-nv-hi** could say would persuade him to stop.

The **ga-no-li-do-hi** turned in defiance toward the **u-ta-so-nv-hi**, but he wasn't there. The **ga-no-li-do-hi** wondered how it could be that the **u-ta-so-nv-hi** could appear and disappear so silently and without his notice. He prided himself on being a more alert and aware **ga-no-li-do-hi**.

46

Soon the **ga-no-li-do-hi** grew drowsy and settled down in the back of his truck for the night. Before he could drift off to sleep, he was fully awakened by a bright glow. He thought that the **u-ta-so-nv-hi** had returned and was shining a lantern in his face. He sat up and opened his eyes.

The glow was coming from the edge of the road. He struggled from his tattered blankets and out of the back of his truck. He hesitated, trying to believe his eyes. His curiosity led him toward the light. A welcoming path that he had not noticed before lay before him, vanishing into the deep woods toward the cliff. The path glowed as if illumined by a full moon, but he was aware that it was a moonless night.

"What is this?" he questioned to himself, unable to resist stepping into the strange scene before him.

The path twisted and turned, and it did not take the **ga-no-li-do-hi** long to realize that he was lost. Strains of beautiful music, mixed with laughter, drifted in and out, first sounding closer then further away as if carried on the breeze. The sounds, always moving, frightened the **ga-no-li-do-hi**. Panicking, he wanted to run back down the path, but it seemed as if the path had changed. It wove itself differently through the trees. Terrified, the **ga-no-li-do-hi** scrambled as fast as he could, tripping over tree roots and stones, scuffing hands and knees, picking himself up and stumbling on until he burst once more into the road and fell toward his truck to secure himself.

He looked toward the **u-ta-so-nv-hi** cabin. Led by the small light in the window he ran onto the porch and pounded on the door. The **u-ta-so-nv-hi** responded as if he had been expecting him. After sharing coffee that he had already prepared and listening to the **ga-no-li-do-hi** story, the **u-ta-so-nv-hi** showed him a fully prepared bed where he was to sleep for the night. The **ga-no-li-do-hi** accepted everything graciously.

The next morning they walked to the camp site. Everything was as he had left it. Then they walked a short distance until the **ga-no-li-do-hi** was sure of the location of the path's entrance. What they saw was an impassable wall of undergrowth.

"I believe you," said the **u-ta-so-nv-hi** grinning. He turned away from the **ga-no-li-do-hi** and headed for his cabin.

The **ga-no-li-do-hi** watched the **u-ta-so-nv-hi** walk away. He looked back at the interweaving of briars and bushes, then looked defeatedly toward the **u-ta-so-nv-hi**. He quickly packed his things and left and was never seen in the Cherokee, **Tsa-la-gi** mountains again.

The trees were full of buds, ready to burst into spring colored leaves. The young people were eager to stay outside as long as they could when weather permitted. This was a day that was hard to let go of when the light faded, especially for a group of playing children and particularly for one boy, **a-tsu-tsa**.

"We have to go in now," one girl, **a-ge-yu-tsa**, stated. "It's getting dark."

"Grandmother, **A-gi-li-si**, said that the Little People, **Yûñ´wi Tsunsdi´**, might come to play with us after dark," said another.

"Strange things might happen," said still another.

"I don't want to go in," said the **a-tsu-tsa**, defying the others. "I don't believe in them anyway."

When he saw the others walking toward the house he pleaded for them to stay, and they begged him to come on in with them. The **a-tsu-tsa**, seeing that he was not going to convince them, plopped down, slumped and grabbed his elbows. He was not going to go.

When he completed his performance, a thorny briar stem struck him across his arm in a loud "whack!" The **a-tsu-tsa** twirled around, by then on his hands and knees. He was ready to smack whoever did this. But nothing was there, not even the briar.

The **a-tsu-tsa** ran inside as fast as he could, passing his friends along the way.

Never Challenge The Little People

*Even for the most contemporary thinker
who sees a majesty and grandeur
in natural law,
sciences cannot explain everything.*

The Elders tell of small voices that can be heard in the woods. Voices that sound like people in conversation or sometimes like whistling or singing. They know to respect these voices, so when they hear such sounds along the trail they silently pass with lowered eyes. They know the voices come from the Little People, **Yûñ´wi Tsunsdi´**.

Sometimes the elders would recall a person who mocked the Little People, **Yûñ´wi Tsunsdi´**. Once a man heard them sing, **ti-no-ge**, and joined in as loud as he could. A bug flew into his mouth and he was coughing and spitting all the way back down the trail.

Another person was trying to dance, **ha-l(a)-sgi**, to their singing and drumming, when his feet got tangled, and he fell into the creek.

Many people have tried to lure the **Yûñ´wi Tsunsdi´** out of hiding by rocking back and forth on their weight stones. They can tell the size of the intruding person by the way the stone tilts. Sometimes they might come to investigate the cause of the disturbance.

The **Yûñ´wi Tsunsdi´** use spider webs to measure a person's height. If you walk low and backwards into a web they might come out to investigate.

The Elders say that if you stop and listen to the small voices while in the woods, the voices will sometimes come to you. They will circle all around you with their laughter and singing, their whistling and chanting. You will find them watching you from behind old stumps and rotting logs, peering out from tree branches and piles of leaves. When this happens, they are the ones who decide when and how you leave. You can't run.

The first green blade of growth had awakened the forest floor. This time of year was long awaited by two young girls, **ta-li a-ni-ge-yu-tsa**, who loved walking through the woods finding unusual and interesting things. Oddly twisted branches, faces in stones, and colored quartz were shared with one of the girl's Grandmother, **A-gi-li-si**, who was always happy to hear of their adventures and to see their treasures.

Entire afternoons spun away at Grandmothers's house, **A-gi-li-si u-we-ne-sv**, as she shared stories about the mountains, legends and Indian wisdoms. But the stories that the **ta-li a-ni-ge-yu-tsa** loved the most were the stories of the Little People, **Yûñ´wi Tsunsdi´**. The **ta-li a-ni-ge-yu-tsa** were intrigued by the caution and reference to forbidden places that always accompanied these stories.

Sunlight, tinged green from new leaves, sifted slowly down through great oaks and young spruce pines made a perfect day for the **ta-li a-ni-ge-yu-tsa** to plunge into the deep woods. Robins, **tsi-sgwo-gwo**,chirped in the branches overhead. Chickadees, **tsi-gi-li-li**, worried the ground in search of tasty spring treats. Squirrels, **sa-lo-li**, scampered through the undergrowth of laurel. The **ta-li a-ni-ge-yu-tsa** felt a pleasant release, anticipating their adventure that had just begun.

After awhile, however, the walk became more difficult. The path grew steeper and last years leaves were damp and slippery. Sharp rose-less briars pulled at their clothes as if trying to stop them or hold them back. The forest grew quiet, and then silent as the girls made their way deeper into the forest.

"We are not suppose to go this far!" one girl, **a-ge-yu-tsa**, said stopping and looking around. After a long disappointed sigh, the other **a-ge-yu-tsa** exclaimed, "We are older now." Since the **ta-li a-ni-ge-yu-tsa** agreed that they had outgrown their warnings, they proceeded further.

They came upon a mass of kudzu with tunneled openings. It reminded them of a hut, and in amazement they went closer and crawled inside. They entered a room made of tree saplings twined tightly together to hold back the invading kudzu vines. The **ta-li a-ni-ge-yu-tsa** stared at the contents. A flat slab of stone was raised off the smooth and trampled floor with a support of handlaced willow. It formed a table which held turtle-shell bowls and carved wooden spoons. Bags made of leather and small clothes hung on the wall. Small honeysuckle baskets held nuts and fresh berries. Everything was small, very small.

Simultaneously the
ta-li a-ni-ge-yu-tsa looked at each
other. Their eyes widened almost as
big as their open mouths. "OOOH!" they
both sounded while not being able to
escape the wide-eyed stare of the other.
"OHHH!" became louder, turning into "AAAH!"
as if the beginning of a chant. Abruptly all that
was heard was the **ta-li a-ni-ge-yu-tsa** scrambling
over each other to reach the outside. They ran as fast
and as far as their breaths would take them.

"Do you think what I think?" one **a-ge-yu-tsa** asked
after stopping to gasp for air. "Yes!" answered the other
a-ge-yu-tsa after stopping and grabbing her shaking knees.
"I think that was one of the forbidden places
A-gi-li-si warned us about.

"What do we do now?"

After a long silence between them the other answered, "Let's go back." The silence became louder; their hearts pounded like drums.

"No."
"Just for a little while."
"No!"

Silence.

"We will just watch ... from a distance."

Silence.

"Promise?"
"Okay, let's go."

One eager and one reluctant **a-ge-yu-tsa,** retraced their steps. The eager one was leading when she heard a desperate groan from behind. She couldn't turn around to see what had happened, because she was frozen by what was in front of her. Neither could move.

He was blocking their way. His long gray hair reached to the ground, and he was dressed like a woodman. His dark brown face held a toothless grin and laughing black eyes. He was scarcely three feet tall. The young girls, **a-ni-ge-yu-tsa-tsa-na-di**, managed to loosen themselves from the shock, turned and ran all the way home.

Arriving in dirty, wet, torn clothes, scratched arms and legs, and skinned knees they related their story to their parents, barely taking a breath until all that had happened was told. Their parents took them immediately to their Grandmother's house, **A-gi-li-so u-we-ne-sv**.

There they stayed for seven days and seven nights. Each daybreak, the **a-ni-ge-yu-tsa-tsa-na-di** would watch **A-gi-li-si** go into the woods carrying a red cloth bundle and return empty handed. Each day at sunset **A-gi-li-si** would talk with the **a-ni-ge-yu-tsa-tsa-na-di** about respect for all living things in the forest.

54

People tell of a man that lived far back in the mountains who was once caught in a sudden thunderstorm, **a-yv-da-gwa-lo-a**. A driving wind, **u-no-le**, and blinding rain, **a-ga-sga**, forced him to seek shelter under a rock ledge near a creek bed. He settled himself down upon a slab of what curiously looked like a small table. Lightening seared the sky above him. He sat listening to the creaking and moaning of the forest, the roaring **a-ga-sga** pulling at the full summer leaves and the rushing of the swelled creek bed. After a time, however, he began to hear something strange.

He listened closely, thinking it was the sound of water rushing over rocks, then more closely, not believing his ears. People were singing, **ka-no-gi-a.** He looked around, trying to determine the direction. He leaned out from under the protective ledge and strained to hear. It was then that he realized that the **ka-no-gi-a** wasn't coming from somewhere around him, but from somewhere underneath him, or, more precisely, underneath the rock he had been using for a seat.

He tried to convince himself it was the voices of the **a-yv-da-gwa-lo-a**, and attempting to relax he gathered his knees with his arms to wait.

"Leave!" cried a voice from under the rock.

The man closed his eyes tightly. "I didn't hear that."

"Leave!" cried the voice again. "Leave or something will happen to you!"

He looked out and saw the rain, **a-ga-sga,** coming down in sheets, lightning and thunder, **a-yv-da-gwa-lo-s,** flashing and clapping all around. He didn't want to leave, but he knew it was the Little People, **Yûñ´wi Tsunsdi´**. Rocks began to fall all around the ledge and then larger rocks clattered closer to him. The man took a deep breath and ran head-long into the **a-yv-da-gwa-lo-a**.

He drudged through the storm without stopping until he reached his cabin, lit a fire and changed his soaked clothes.

"The **Yûñ´wi Tsunsdi´**, have always helped me," he thought. "They must have had a real strong need for me to leave to send me out into such a ferocious **a-yv-da-gwa-lo-a**!"

A cold autumn morning found a young woodcutter, **a-di sgwa-lv-sgi,** chopping wood in his backyard. The past few days of his life had not been pleasant, and so he was in a foul mood. He grumbled and fussed with each raising of the ax, **ga-lu-sdi,** and with each loud cut, **a-tsa-k(a)-sdi.** Grumble and **a-tsa-k(a)-sdi,** grumble and **a-tsa-k(a)-sdi.** The grumbling became louder with each heavy blow. The **ga-lu-sdi** raised higher with each grumble. Finally, he raised the **ga-lu-sdi** with a huge bellow and swung down hard. The **ga-lu-sdi** glanced off the log and spun out of his hands toward the woods.

There, at the edge of the wood, stood a man with long dark hair and dark skin looking back at the angry young man. The **ga-lu-sdi** leaned up against a tree beside him, and the woodcutter, **a-di sgwa-lv-sgi,** could tell that the man was no taller than the **ga-lu-sdi** was long.

"How long have you been standing there?" he asked the tiny fellow. The little man just stared at him with an unreadable expression on his face. "What are you doing here?" He asked again. "What do you want?" But the little man did not respond. Already in an ill temper, he was in no mood for nonsense. He ran into his house to get his shotgun.

When he returned, the little man was gone. The **a-di sgwa-lv-sgi** looked all around the edge of his yard, but he could find no trace of the mysterious stranger. Finally, he gave up and went to get his **ga-lu-sdi.**

Beside the **ga-lu-sdi** he found a tattered bag full of pecans. He stared at them for a long time. Pecans were his favorite kind of nut and they could not be found in the mountains.

The **a-di sgwa-lv-sgi** glanced at his shotgun and wondered if he would have used it. He munched a few pecans and sat down for a while to think. His black mood passed. He ate a few more and became thankful for having wood to keep his family warm. The more he ate the more appreciative he became. Eventually, he found he could not even remember what had upset him so much. That night he went to bed content, and he savored his rare gift for many days.

Cherokee
Medicine
People

and the
Yuñwi Tsunsdi'

You have to be blind to see
and deaf to hear.
Let go of logic from mere intelligence
to know what really is truth.

Little People, **Yûñ´wi Tsunsdi´**, are an example of the life power that is in nature.

If adults or children have the right qualifications and talent the **Yûñ´wi Tsunsdi´** sometimes steal them away from the world to teach them. (As in the story "A Child is Born" - page 26).

The **Yûñ´wi Tsunsdi´** can do anything they want, but usually a child is not taught as much as an adult.

The **Yûñ´wi Tsunsdi´** base their beliefs of life, love and pleasure on the cycles of nature and the rhythms of the universe. Their belief is one of balance. Within their rituals are found music, dance, song, and laughter — lots of laughter. They have a life-oriented religion.

Yûñ´wi Tsunsdi´ have no beliefs or "religion" as it is categorized today. A belief is sometimes limiting, whereas the truths of life and nature and the knowledge of the Great Spirit is limitless. Their "religion" is life itself — the acceptance of "what is" and meeting it with love. Love sometimes means correcting or showing real power and reasoning, greater than human understanding, for the sake of restoring balance, peace, and harmony.

They do not practice "collective decisions," made by humans, as a way of determining behavior. They agree that all must live within laws, but nature's laws. They would never argue, or divide themselves, about the truths of the Great Spirit. Their behavior is determined by their oneness with all things and the Giver of Life.

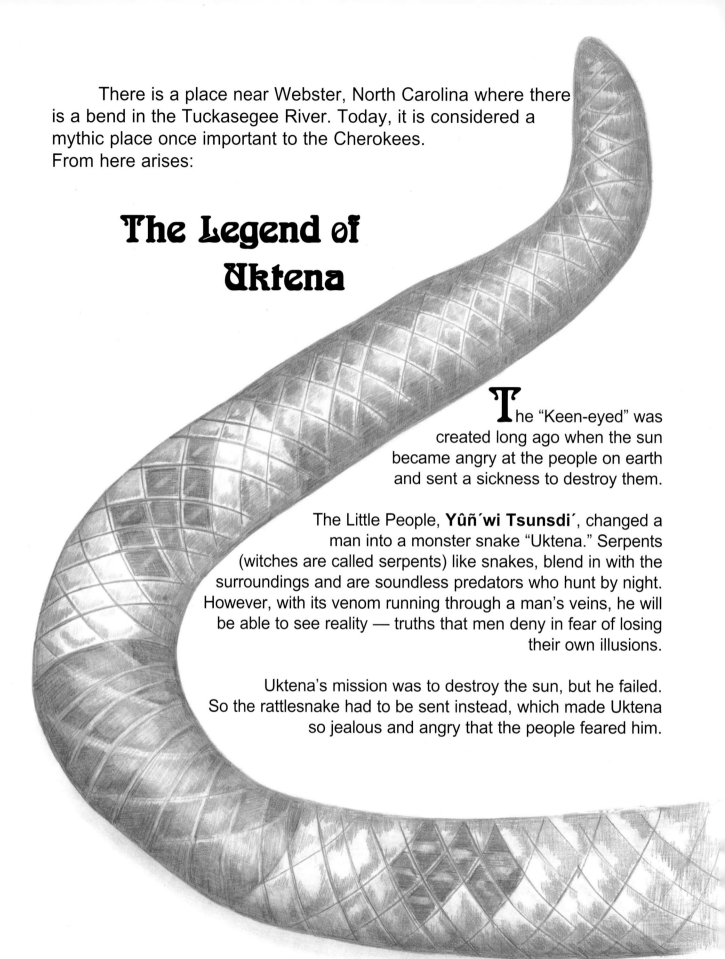

There is a place near Webster, North Carolina where there is a bend in the Tuckasegee River. Today, it is considered a mythic place once important to the Cherokees. From here arises:

The Legend of Uktena

The "Keen-eyed" was created long ago when the sun became angry at the people on earth and sent a sickness to destroy them.

The Little People, **Yûñ´wi Tsunsdi´**, changed a man into a monster snake "Uktena." Serpents (witches are called serpents) like snakes, blend in with the surroundings and are soundless predators who hunt by night. However, with its venom running through a man's veins, he will be able to see reality — truths that men deny in fear of losing their own illusions.

Uktena's mission was to destroy the sun, but he failed. So the rattlesnake had to be sent instead, which made Uktena so jealous and angry that the people feared him.

Eventually, the first Uktena was captured and taken to a place where dangerous things are kept — but not before there were other Uktenas around, hiding in deep pools of rivers and in lonely passes of the higher mountains. This not so peaceful place was the bend in the Tuckasegee

The Uktena was no small enemy. This snake was as large around as a tree, with horns on its head, and a bright blazing crest like a diamond upon his forehead, and scales glittering like sparks of fire," the Uktena had rings or spots of color along its whole body length and could not be wounded except by shooting it in the "seventh spot' from the head, because under this spot is where lies its heart and its life. The spot which is called "Ulunsu´ti" in Cherokee and means "transparent or blazing diamond," was worth aiming for but dangerous to attempt. Anyone seen by the Uktena would become so dazed by the light from the Ulunsuti that he would run toward the snake instead of trying to escape.

If one did manage to kill the Uktena and gain the Ulunsu'´ti, then success in hunting, love, rainmaking and every other activity was assured. Possessing the Ulunsu'ti also brought the gift of prophecy. The owner could consult the Ulunsu'ti about the future and see it mirrored in the crystal. He would know whether a sick man would recover, whether a warrior would return from battle or whether he would live to be old, for instance.

Hunting the Uktena was a difficult task. Even if one managed to get close enough without being seen by the giant snake-monster, gazing upon it while it slept brought death — not to the hunter, but to his family.

Many daring Cherokee tried to conquer the Uktena but the only person to succeed was Agan-uni´tsi, "The Groundhog Mother." (Meaning: a tender heart for the orphaned young); he once mothered an orphaned groundhog.

Agan-uni´tsi's search for the Uktena began after a Cherokee battle with the Shawnee who were all considered "magicians." The Cherokee captured a great medicine man, Agan-uni´tsi. To plead for his life he promised that, if spared, he would find, for the Cherokees, the Ulunsu´ti, or, the blazing star in the forehead of the Uktena.

While the Cherokee knew that possession of the Ulunsu´ti meant marvelous abilities became available, they also knew that even meeting the Uktena could mean sudden death. They warned Agan-uni´tsi, but he answered that his medicine was strong and he was not afraid. So the deal was made. It was a long search and Agan-uni´tsi met many giant creatures along the way that meant to weaken his faith before he found Uktena asleep on a mountaintop.

Turning without noise, he ran swiftly down the mountainside as fast as he could go with one long breath. He ran nearly to the bottom of the slope. There he stopped and piled a great circle of pine cones, and inside he dug a deep trench. Then he set fire to the cones and came back to the mountaintop.

61

The Uktena was still asleep, and putting an arrow to his bow, Agan-uni´tsi shot and sent the arrow through its heart, which was under the seventh spot from the serpent's head.

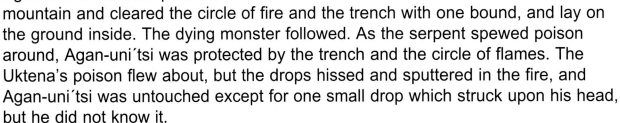

The snake raised its head, flashed fire and started toward the medicine man, but Agan-uni´tsi ran full speed down the mountain and cleared the circle of fire and the trench with one bound, and lay on the ground inside. The dying monster followed. As the serpent spewed poison around, Agan-uni´tsi was protected by the trench and the circle of flames. The Uktena's poison flew about, but the drops hissed and sputtered in the fire, and Agan-uni´tsi was untouched except for one small drop which struck upon his head, but he did not know it.

The Uktena's dark blood ran into the trench but did not touch the medicine man. Finally, the dead serpent rolled over and over down the mountain, breaking trees until it stopped at the bottom. Seven days later Agan-uni´tsi went, at night, to the spot where the Uktena's carcass lay. The bright light of the Ulunsu´ti was easy to spot in the darkness, and the medicine man collected it from a low hanging branch where a raven had dropped it. He carefully wrapped it and took it home.

From that time he became the greatest medicine man in the whole tribe. In later years, when Agan-uni´tsi came into the settlement, people did notice that hanging from his head, on the spot where the single drop of Uktena's poison had struck, was a small snake. But for as long as he lived, he himself, never knew that it was there.

This is the knowledge the medicine men often refer to: remember the great power and reasoning of the Little People. The Little People know the path of their transformation, the reasoning behind it and the purpose.

"I have found that a sickness lies in wait for Little People of Power — a soul sickness. It eats and eats at even the most devoted. When you can see through the moss-covered pool of the world to the rocks lying on the bottom, you begin to wonder why the pool exists at all. What purpose is served by making it hard for humans to see the rocks? Why doesn't Power just make all pools clear, or drain them away so the rocks are easily visible? I understand that this is why contraries and tricksters are made.

The bottom of the pool is invisible. So someone must pick up the rocks and throw them at people, because only a good bash to the brain will make a human stop rushing long enough to consider standing on his head for a better look around — and this includes all with power. But it hurts just the same. Bashing and being bashed.

Yes, it hurts ... the pain of those near me increases every day, and I feel their suffering like a disease inside me, sapping my strength, filling me with questions, sometimes with rage or grief — and all I can do is keep throwing rocks."

Medicine people have encounters with the Little People, **Yûñ´wi Tsunsdi´**, often. They talk about the plants, **a-su-lo**, and their cures and discuss remedies. Medicine people know where and how to find the **Yûñ´wi Tsunsdi´**.

If a medicine person can not go to the woods for the **a-su-lo** he needs the **Yûñ´wi Tsunsdi´** often bring the **a-su-lo** to him.

Sometimes, the **Yûñ´wi Tsunsdi´** just come to visit, sit down, stay awhile but say nothing. Sooner or later the message the medicine person needs is understood.

At times the medicine person does not know he needs a message. The **Yûñ´wi Tsunsdi´** always know.

A baby, **u-sdi** cried. "Where is that young mother, **e-tsi**?" a voice rose from a huddled group of women, **a-ni-ge-ya**, busy preparing a meal. "Does any one see her?" No one answered but heads turned looking around. One by one the **a-ni-ge-ya** began leaving in search for her. "Who saw her last?" inquired one of the grandmothers, **a-gi-li-si**. No one had seen her for a while.

A woman holding the crying baby watched the **A-gi-li-si** hurry over to the men gathered under a large locust tree. Their talking subsided when they saw **A-gi-li-si** lean over and whisper something to one of the elders whose medicine skills included the ability to find things and people.

The elder nodded his head implying that he understood what **A-gi-li-si** had told him.

He thumbed into his vest pocket and withdrew an old buckskin pouch. Retrieving a diamond shaped crystal he clutched it in the palm of his hand and mumbled something indistinguishable. He then opened his hand and stared into the stone. Without expression he whispered back to **A-gi-li-si**, and then turned his attention back to the other men.

The **A-gi-li-si** hurried back and called for three **a-ni-ge-ya** to accompany her, and they trailed off into the woods. They found the lost **E-tsi** where the elder had said she would be. She was sitting on a large rock, her clothes soaked from her waist down, her eyes unfocused, and her gaze unsteady. The **A-gi-li-si** approached her slowly. She put her hand softly on her head and spoke her name. As if a spell had been broken, the **E-tsi** looked from one to the other of her friends. She laughed and hugged each one.

"Are you all right?" asked one of the **a-ni-ge-ya**. "Oh yes," she said spilling immediately into all the good things she had just experienced. "I had apples to eat," she said, "and peaches, strawberries, grapes and plums." The **a-ni-ge-ya** looked back and forth at each other. "Apples you say?" **A-gi-li-si** asked curiously. One of the **a-ni-ge-ya** looked inquisitively at **A-gi-li-si**, but **A-gi-li-si** quickly nodded at the woman indicating that she knew that apples were not in season.

The woman remained silent as she helped the **E-tsi** stand. As if needing to explain she said, "My clothes are wet because we had to cross a deep creek to get back." "We?" one of the **a-ni-ge-ya** asked looking around and up and down the trail. "Oh, they have gone now," the girl said reassuring the anxious **a-ni-ge-ya**. "And we had better do the same," said **A-gi-li-si**, as she headed her charges toward home.

As soon as they returned, **A-gi-li-si** went straight to the elder and informed him how the girl told about being with the Little People, **Yûñ´wi Tsunsdi´**. The smiles they exchanged reassured **A-gi-li-si** that nothing would happen to the young **E-tsi**, and nothing did!

65

Some Cherokee, **Tsa-la-gi**, elders know secret formulas, and there have been many in the past who had their own. The formulas were sometimes used to protect the **Tsa-la-gi** homes, livestock and crops while they were away. They also used their formulas to help people who were sick or who needed protection.

Once, a man who was a conjuror and had a secret formula was leaving his home for a while and wanted to protect his house.

Early, on the morning he was leaving on his trip, he went into the woods and gathered what he needed to make his medicine. After bringing it home he began to smoke his house using a special dried plant. Only then could he begin to prepare his formula. He made a mixture of herbs he gathered from the woods then prepared his pipe, **a-hu-tsa-wo-do-ti**, and filled it with Indian tobacco, **tso-la**, and other assisting plants, **a-su-lo**. He took some regular **tso-la** from its container to "remake" it.

He performed his ritual with a chant while taking all these things and placing them directly on the ground, ending with another chant. (The combination of the whole procedure is known as a "secret formula.")

The man knew that sometimes the spirits did not come right away. When this happened theLittle People, **Yûñ´wi Tsunsdi´**, would come and smoke his **a-hu-tsa-wo-do-ti**, use the "remade" **tso-la** and take his medicine to someone who needed it.

The secret formula must be done correctly or neither will come to help. Apparently the man must have been anxious to leave and missed something, because when he returned his house had burned to the ground.

Two men were headed up the mountain near Big Witch Community to a secret place where one of them had experienced some interesting and unusual happenings when he was a child. He had invited his friend to go with him to this special place.

As they passed a formation of flat rocks stacked on top of one another, the friend asked about it.

"Nobody knows. Some say it could be an old furnace, **a-ga-no-di-sk**," he replied and walked ahead at a faster pace.

As his friend passed by the stone "**a-ga-no-di-sk**," he slowed down to examine the odd looking structure. Suddenly, something tugged at his pants leg. He looked down, expecting it to be a briar, but there was nothing there. As he started to continue on, perplexed, it happened again even harder than before. He could see and feel his pants being tugged with no apparent reason.

Frightened, he hurried along to catch up with his friend, who was now further up the mountain resting under an old cherry tree. "Did anything happen when you passed that pile of rocks?" he heard his friend ask as he caught up with him. "Yes!" his friend replied curtly, "What was that?"

As they rested under the tree, he shared with him the reason behind the strange tugging phenomena. "Well," he said, "when I was a youngster I would come here with my Grandfather, **E-du-du**, who was a medicine man, **di-da-nv-wi-sgi**. He would always take his leather bag containing herbs, healing roots and a twist of tobacco, **tso-la,** with him. He would leave the bag on the same stone by the **a-ga-no-di-sk** each time, then we would come on up here to this old tree and rest for a while. When we went back for the bag, it would always be empty. When I got oldrer my **E-du-du** told me that the medicine and **tso-la** were for the Little People, **Yûñ´wi Tsunsdi´**, who lived there. Anyone who comes here since my **E-du-du** quit coming often feels the tug of the **Yûñ´wi Tsunsdi´** as they pass the rocks."

It was a rush against time on a good fishing day. Packing the gear and getting to his favorite fishing hole was all that one Cherokee had on his mind. He barely made it to the head of Raven Creek by the time daylight crept in. He found a suitable rock to sit on to enjoy the cool grayness of the morning before he dropped his line. He enjoyed hearing the sounds of the forest waking up.

His calm was disturbed as he heard a strange noise. He sat up straight and looked around but couldn't see anything. He heard it again and searched in the direction of the sound. "Oh! It's you; come on over," he said as he waved his hand. Approaching were two mid-age men dressed for the cool mountain morning. They had long black hair and smiling faces. They were about three feet tall.

"Are you fishing here today?" asked the fisherman.

"No," they answered. "We have come to take you with us."

The man rose, laughing, and teased, "On my fishing day?"

They all three had exchanged jest and cheerful greetings when the man said, "Well, lead the way!"

The Little People, **Yûñ´wi Tsunsdi´**, took him a short distance into the forest when a path, **wa-ga-lo-hi-sdi**, appeared. It was clear of stones, tree roots and other obstacles, making it easy to walk.

The **wa-ga-lo-hi-sdi** led far into the mountains through many beautiful flowers and blooming rhododendron, and songbirds sang as they enjoyed their walk. Abruptly, the **wa-ga-lo-hi-sdi** ended with a huge boulder blocking the way.

"Follow us," the **Yûñ´wi Tsunsdi´** said, encouraging him through a narrow crevice. The man was having difficulty squeezing through when they told him to keep trying. Suddenly he slipped right through. It seemed as if the crevice had grown wider to allow him entrance.

Darkness met him on the inside and he could not see. Strains of laughter and the delightful aroma of food led him forward to a large well-lit room of a cave where other **Yûñ´wi Tsunsdi´** were all around preparing a meal.

Being a medicine man, **di-da-nv-wi-sgi,** and and having met with the **Yûñ´wi Tsunsdi´** often, he was not surprised when they offered him a coiled rattlesnake, for a chair.

68

A Cherokee dish of beans and hominy, **se-lu di-su-ye**, was served. He was given a carved horn to use as a spoon, but with each attempt to eat, the food would fall from the spoon before it reached his mouth. However, he grew less and less hungry and soon became very satisfied.

After the meal, the pipe, **a-hu-tsa-wo-do-ti**, was brought out, and the man stayed with them for two days discussing herbs, plants, and roots used for healing. The man learned far more than he had ever known, and the **Yûñ´wi Tsunsdi´** wanted him to take the knowledge and use it for his tribe. They also told him that his time was short, and that he would pass to the next world before the next full moon.

When the meeting was over the **di-da-nv-wi-sgi** thanked them by leaving tobacco, **tso-la**, as was the custom.

Upon returning to his home the man taught his son everything, and upon his death he was wrapped in a special blanket, put into a wooden box and carried high on a mountaintop according to his request.

The son became a great **di-da-nv-wi-sgi** for his tribe.

Did you hear that? Did you hear that?" frantically repeated the old medicine man, **di-danv-wi-sgi**, as he met one of his neighbors, **na-v e-hi**, along the road.

"Hear what?" his **na-v e-hi** inquired.

"That loud boom!" he stuttered over his answer while repeating it.

His **na-v e-hi** naturally looked up. The sun was bright in a clear blue sky. A few wispy clouds drifted overhead. It was a calm day. "Are you talking about thunder, **a-yv-da-gwa-lo-s**?" he asked.

"No, well yes, maybe! Come see!" the old man stammered as he drug him back down the road.

As they came around the curve of the road, both stopped and stared at a huge tree. The whole top had exploded and shattered into pieces.

"What happened?" the **na-vi e-hi** asked, hoping for a simple explanation.

"I was passing under the tree when a loud boom sounded. The top was falling toward me, and I ran."

For a while they both stood examining the rubble while their hearts beat like a pot drum.

"I might have been conjured on," he soon said very softly.

"What do you mean?" his **na-v e-hi** asked.

Not answering directly, he began, "Through time there have been some medicine men, **di-na-da-nv-wi-sgi**, that were jealous of other **di-na-da-nv-wi-sgi** and wanted to scare them away from their medicine. Sometimes jealous people would go to a medicine man, **di-da-nv-wi-sgi**, enlisting him to do ill things to others. Sometimes the **di-da-nv-wi-sgi** would use the power of the Little People, **Yûñ´wi Tsunsdi´**, because their own power was weak." He paused. "This looks like the power of the **Yûñ´wi Tsunsdi´**."

"Do you know the **di-da-nv-wi-sgi** behind this?" his friend asked with concern.

"Maybe!" but the old man said no more and quietly walked away.

However, the **Yûñ´wi Tsunsdi´** teach us this lesson:

"Be assured that if you hurt someone, or even try to hurt them, for any reason, it will always come back on you or a member of your family."

This is just another of the mysterious ways of the **Yûñ´wi Tsunsdi´**.

"**Y**ou can't learn much riding in a wagon," an old medicine man, **di-da-nv-wi-sgi**, was telling his grandson. They were walking home from Sunday church together. Some wagons had passed them by and each time they were offered a ride. The dust, stirred up from the wagons, was beginning to settle on the dirt road stripped with ruts and riddled with potholes. The boy slipped his hand into Grandfather's, **E- du-du**, as they watched them go out of sight.

On warm sunny days they walked home, and it was always interesting listening to what **E-du-du** had to say. His "religion" came from nature. He called it the "natural order of things".

"This way!" he heard his **E-du-du** say as they went off the road and down an embankment to the creek. The boy did not hesitate. He always followed his **E-du-du** everywhere. "Sit here," his **E-du-du** pointed to a fallen tree next to the water. They both were seated when **E-du-du** said, "Now tell me, what do you see?"

The boy had, in the past, learned that nature wasn't what it seemed while enjoying a nice casual view. Most everywhere in the mountains there was a nice view. Nature had to be learned by viewing one life at a time, a plant or large tree, a pebble or a boulder, the ways of water, the life in the ground, wondering, touching, feeling until understanding came. Today they would listen, **s-dv-da-sde-sdi**.

They sat for a long time, feeling the sun and listening as if their eyes were closed. Finally his **E-du-du** asked, "Did you hear that?"

"What?" questioned the boy.

E-du-du didn't reply. After a while **E-du-du** said again, "There it is. Did you hear that?"

Squinting, the boy looked around and again asked, "What?"

E-du-du noticed him squinting and reminded him, "You can't hear with your eyes!"

There was silence between them until: "I heard it, **E-du-du**. Someone is calling you. They are saying your Indian name! It's coming from the woods across the creek."

Only a few people called **E-du-du** by his Indian name anymore.

E-du-du was laughing as the boy, **a-tsu-tsa**, was waving his hand as hard as he could, keeping his eyes on the top of a hemlock. He told the **a-tsu-tsa** that they had to be still and keep very quiet. The **a-tsu-tsa** obliged with a big smile on his face. **E-du-du** was no longer smiling, he sat quietly watching a little man watch him. Soon he nudged the **a-tsu-tsa** to get his attention and gave a nod toward the road. It was time to go. The **a-tsu-tsa** looked back to the hemlock. The little man was gone.

E-du-du, the **a-tsu-tsa** and his mother, **e-tsi**, all lived together and every Sunday she would have extra good food waiting for them when they returned. The **a-tsu-tsa** daydreamed about what it was going to be today. He was very hungry. He knew **E-du-du** must be hungry too because they headed straight home—no more stops and no more talking.

But **E-du-du** did not eat when he got home; he went straight to the tool shed. He started tightening down planks in the chicken house, moving barrels around the corral and filling them with water to make them heavy. Next, he put the pigs in a sapling-pen that he used when he wanted to fatten them. It was all so strange, because **E-du-du** never worked on Sunday.

That night the wind began to blow. It blew stronger and stronger. The **a-tsu-tsa** could hear tree limbs breaking. Large limbs were hitting the barn and smashing against the house. The howl of the wind was deafening. From underneath his **E-du-du** arm the wide-eyed **a-tsu-tsa** watched his **E-tsi** mending their clothes. **E-du-du** was calmly enjoying his corncob pipe.

"Did that little man we saw tell you that the winds were coming?"

E-du-du nodded his head and smiled.

73

A family in Birdtown was troubled by the Little People, **Yûñ´wi Tsunsdi´**. Frequently, at night, they heard banging and thumping. Often, when it sounded like things were being moved around, they could see mysterious shadows. During the day they could hear singing and laughing and chatter that no one could understand. Once, the family got bombarded with dobs of dirt coming from the roof of their cabin, **a-da-ne-lv**.

The **a-da-ne-lv**, was small. One room served as a bedroom, living room and kitchen. The meals were cooked in an open fireplace at one end. Above was a loft that kept food such as dried beans, canned fruits and vegetables, salted meat, barrels of flour and cornmeal. It also had a corncrib to store dried ears of corn.

Sometimes the family would hear the **Yûñ´wi Tsunsdi´** walking around in the loft. Late at night they would throw corn cobs down the ladder steps or drop blades of fodder on the family below.

People would come to the **a-da-ne-lv** to stay with the family a day or two just to witness these strange events. Many of them offered advice on what to do about the **Yûñ´wi Tsunsdi´**. Nothing worked. They would not go away.

Finally, the family heard of a medicine man, **di-da-nv-wi-sgi**, who could banish unwanted spirits. They were hoping that he could do something with the **Yûñ´wi Tsunsdi´**. The family made ready for the journey to bring him to the **a-da-ne-lv**. They packed gifts of blankets, quilts, food and a pig.

Upon arriving at the **Di-da-nv-wi-sgi** house, the family placed a twist of tobacco, **tso-la**, on his table, which was the custom. His taking it would indicate his willingness to do what they wanted. He listened in silence to their story. The **tso-la** was still on the table when the family left to make camp in his yard. The next day the **tso-la** was gone, and the **Di-da-nv-wi-sgi** was packed and waiting on the porch. Everyone hurried to make the journey home.

They arrived late, and after eating, they all went to bed except the **Di-da-nv-wi-sgi**. He put food, some of everything they had eaten for supper, out on the front porch. He sat in a rocking chair beside the fireplace and rocked all night, watching the smoke and listening to the dry wood crackle.

The next day they all ate and made preparations for the return trip. Again, the man put food on the porch. The family returned home late the next day and went immediately to bed. They slept soundly without the usual noises. From that time on it was peaceful around their house.

Tragedy and joy,
light and dark,
neither side seeing the whole.
Their war is everlasting.
Perhaps that is the unalterable truth.

I keep praying—
watching—
thinking—
that a bridge must exist,
a bridge that stretches above the war
not to be captured on either side.

Opposites crossed,
Standing in the middle
you can see both sides
—-but not the bridge,
just the endless conflict.
The elders speak of the Mysterious
One's quiet soul.

I wonder if this is not the bridge.

Deep inside...
on the edge of my knowing
I already know ... I just haven't seen.

There was a time that native people raided each other's villages, took food and livestock and captured women as potential brides. They often fought over boundaries and rights to disputed lands. Acts of bravery and skill were measured within these raids, but the cost of lives of leaders and families was at a minimum. Pride was more at stake than lives on both sides.

The intensity of warfare changed as warriors, **a-ni-yv-wi-ya-hi,** went on expeditions with the intent to kill for the sole reason of protecting their land from the encroaching Europeans.

The families at home listened for the Little People, **Yûñ´wi Tsunsdi´**, to tell them what was happening with their **a-ni-yv-wi-ya-hi**.

If the people heard a war hoop and the sound was extended, Cherokee, **Tsa-la-gi**, **a-ni-yv-wi-ya-hi** were killing the invaders. If the sound was short the **a-ni-yv-wi-ya-hi** were getting killed.

The medicine men, **di-na-da-nv-wi-sgi**, were the ones to translate for the people. But during the dark times of the removal, known as the Trail of Tears, the **Yûñ´wi Tsunsdi´** stayed close and warned the families themselves of victory or defeat or the death of their sons or daughters.

77

What Is A Medicine Man
(Indian Doctor)

Medicine People, both men and women, have special knowledge. They know about their own spirits as well as the spirits of animals, birds, insects, plants, trees, water and the inhabitants of water. They know that all spirits are interconnected and can relate to one another, living together respectfully as they both need and help one another.

For example, a medicine man, **di-da-nv-wi-sgi**, who has a special relationship with the plant spirits which have healing properties, can enhance the power of the plant to heal illnesses.

Medicine men, **di-na-da-nv-wi-sgi** understand the "natural order of things," being in perfect balance with each other and they know that people are a part of that.

Whereas nature works instinctively, people work with perception, how they perceive things. Unclear and limited perceptions create a difference. Limitations and good or bad action toward other people, grow out of perceptions. So do the many talents, enabling some to be exceptional with plants, **a-su-lo**, and healing while others are able to find lost people and things. Some are able to tell of things to occur in the future, while others are apt at shape-changing.

Of the many different talents and combinations of talents, the most sought after is the ability to help with sicknesses. **Di-na-da-nv-wi-sgi** who have this ability are often called Indian Doctors, **Yv-wi-ya V-da-nv-wi-sgi.**

The word "conjuror" was given to the medicine people by non-Indians, because they witnessed their ability to "change things" or "conjure."

All things
are real,
yet there is so much reality
we do not know.

CHEROKEE
CHILDREN
and the
Yuñwi Tsunsdi'

Sometimes adults want life's battles to be taken away from them. So it is with children also. It is not realized while we are growing physically and emotionally that only in the struggling with the shadows is the Light made manifest.

Many stories are told of encounters between children and Little People from ancient times to the present.

The Little People and the children enjoy each other. One does not threaten the other. It is said that Little People talk to the children about animals and nature.

Children have many questions about their new world. They are not interested in gossip and bad behavior, and they care little for opinions, attitudes or problems.

But, they are curious about the truth of things, from the tiny insects in the earth to the great stars in a black night.

The Little People want the minds of children to grow well and to develop important concepts of truth. They show them wonderful things and continue to remind and instruct them until they grow to a certain age.

It was the time of strawberries, **a-ni**. A young girl, almost ten years old, was anxious to get to the trail that would lead her to where the berries were ripe and juicy and red. Her brother knew where she was going when he saw her with her gathering basket gripped tightly in her hand. He warned her, "Don't go near the cave on the other side of the mountain. The Little People, **Yûñ´wi Tsunsdi´**, live there." His warning faded, as she did, into the woods.

She found the **a-ni**, where she knew they would be and started jumping around like a rabbit in springtime, grabbing all that she could see. Eventually, her basket was full, and **a-ni** juice dripped off her chin. Her dress was spotted with red where the juice oozed from her full basket, and it was evident that she had enough.

On the way home, **di-gwe-nv-sv**, she spotted more **a-ni** a good distance from the trail and climbed to pick those too. When she tasted them, they were the most delicious yet, and she couldn't help climbing further and further for more berries leading her deeper and deeper into the forest. When she couldn't eat another one, and her cupped dress was as full as her basket, she started home again, except this time she didn't know which way to go. She could no longer see the trail. She walked a short way in one direction and then another. Realizing that she was lost she sat down on a nearby rock, frightened, and buried her face in her hands trying to hold back the tears. All thoughts of **a-ni** had vanished.

"Hello," came a voice, sounding like that of a grown woman, directly in front of her. It startled her.

"Who are you?" she asked.

"I live in that cave on the other side of the mountain."

"Are you one of the **Yûñ´wi Tsunsdi´**? You're so small."

"Yes, are you the one who took all the **a-ni**?"

The girl was so happy to see someone, especially an adult. Other **Yûñ´wi Tsunsdi´** gathered around her with empty baskets as she offered to share her **a-ni**.

"Would you like to come with us and share your berries with the rest of our village?" asked the woman..

85

The girl was so relieved to be found, that she readily agreed. At this point she would have shared with anyone, even her brother if only he was here.

The **Yûñ´wi Tsunsdi´** filled their empty baskets and helped her carry her many **a-ni** to a secluded cave. Inside, other **Yûñ´wi Tsunsdi´** were eating from a big table filled with food from all seasons. She ate and ate and shared her **a-ni** until everyone was full and the food was gone. She barely noticed sleep closing her eyes.

She awoke to music and saw the table full again. The **Yûñ´wi Tsunsdi´** were feasting and dancing. Again, she joined the festivities and had a wonderful time, but eventually she grew tired and longed for home, **di-gwe-nv-sv**. The **Yûñ´wi Tsunsdi´** did not want her to go, but, knowing she was homesick, they led her back to the trail.

"Wait!" she said, "This is not the trail. It looks different." Brush and briar had intertwined with fallen trees across the trail.

"Yes, it is!" They finally convinced her that it would lead her **di-gwe-nv-sv**.

Eventually, it did. She arrived **di-gwe-nv-sv** and slipped timidly through the back door, hoping to avoid her brother who was sure to tease her about returning without berries for every-one. Keeping her eyes lowered, she went into the room where she knew her family would be having dinner. All eyes were on her in amazement. She took her place at the table and jumped a little as her mother, **E-tsi**, screamed and rushed to hug her. Her grandmother, **A-gi-li-si**, dropped a dish and it broke all over the floor. She even caught a glimpse of tears in her brother's eyes.

"Are you all mad at me for staying gone all day and not returning with **a-ni**?" she asked, turning to her father.

"**A-ni**? What **a-ni**?" he asked, "And you haven't been gone all day, you've been gone for several years." She was stunned that years of her life could have passed away without her knowing it.

Her **A-gi-li-si** was very curious and kept pressing her for information until finally, she told everything. Her **A-gi-li-si** was upset,because she knew what it meant to tell about being with the **Yûñ´wi Tsunsdi´**. Soon the girl became very ill.

The **A-gi-li-si** would hardly let anyone else take care of her. The girl was sick a long time. When her **A-gi-li-si** took flowers to her grave, she would always find beautiful fresh flowers already there. They were left by the **Yûñ´wi Tsunsdi´**.

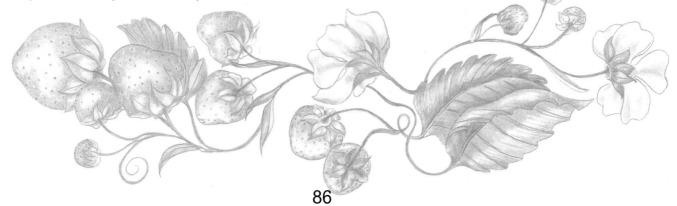

86

ong ago, after the removal, known as *The Trail of Tears*, times were hard, farms and crops had been burned by the soldiers, and families often had to scavenge the woods for food. One day a Cherokee, **Tsa-la-gi**, man, his wife and young son were in the forest searching for roots to eat when the young son disappeared. The mother, **e-tsi**, became frantic. The father, **a-gi-do-da**, searched the forest for days and days, but signs of the little boy could not be found. Hope grew slim as the heavy winter, **go-la**, settled in, isolated the couple and kept them hungry. The couple barely survived.

Go-la broke and spring, **go-ge-yi**, came. Still sad and sorrow stricken. Emotions were numbed from the months of want, the **e-tsi** went into the mountains to gather what the spring-time forest had to offer.

"Momma, **E-tsi**?"

The **e-tsi** held her bent head and cried at what she heard.

"**E-tsi**! I was just on my way to find you."

She raised her head to the direction of the voice and froze. There, sitting on a rock, engulfed in rays of sunshine, was her son. He was healthy and plump with ruddy cheeks that gave way to a grand smile.

Her young son held his arms out for her to take him. She walked slowly toward him not believing what she was seeing. Holding her hand out as far as she could reach, tears streaking down her dusty face, she reluctantly reached to touch his little fingers, so afraid she was dreaming. They touched. She grabbed him and drew him to her, holding him tightly for a long time. He felt real and warm, and his arms clasped around her neck.

The mother, so weak, sat humbled back down on the rock not daring to let him out of her touch while she asked him about his disappearance.

"I've been with the Little People, **Yûñ´wi Tsunsdi**," he said, trying to comfort her. "I stayed warm and I never got hungry, because they fed me crawfish, **tsiska- gili** ."

From a distance the father saw his wife returning, carrying a large bundle.

"Oh, no," he said out loud, trying to hold on to his acceptance that his son was gone to avoid his pain renewing. He ran to meet his wife almost knocking her over as his arms went around them both. She was truely carrying their son. He cried.

The father had rabbit stew boiling in a skin pouch while they listened to their son. He told them that the **Yûñ´wi Tsunsdi´**, had promised that their family would never be hungry again. After eating, the boy insisted that they go down by the creek. There they saw the red **tsiska- gili** that they could eat. An endless supply.

The mountains were locked in the grip of winter, **go-la**, at Sherrill's Cove, the snow had blown and drifted deep. Every child, and child-at-heart, braced for the chill and grabbed a sled, can lid, old sheet of tin or an old wash tub and headed for the ice-crusted hillside. A big bonfire was built for warmth and everyone enjoyed the fun.

For weeks before, the children had tried to be good and helpful, hoping that the Little People, **Yûñ´wi Tsunsdi´**, would favor them during their **go-la** sledding. Many believed that the **Yûñ´wi Tsunsdi´** could make them go fast or slow, tip them over, spin them around or cause them to win or lose a race.

The Sherrill Cove sled run finishes at a creek where the **Yûñ´wi Tsunsdi´** are known to be. The fastest sled sometimes stopped short before plunging into the water, and sometimes the very slowest sled plunged right into the creek in spite of everything anyone could do to prevent it.

The last school bell, **ka-lv-na**, rang early that day and the doors to the school, **tsu-na-de-lo qwa-sdi**, burst open with a stream of children. Snow fell like goose down. It already lay thick upon the ground and more accumulation was expected. A group of neighborhood friends gathered outside to walk home together as on any other day.

The group had thinned to a few when the brother, **a-gi-do**, looked around and realized that his little sister, **u-sdi a-gi-lv**, was missing. No one seemed to know what had happened to her. They all ran back down the road calling her name, but she did not answer. Her **a-gi-do** ran home as quickly as he could and informed his parents of her disappearance.

Many of the neighbors joined in the hunt, and they all searched into the dark night with no success.

Early the next morning one of the men was standing on a largeboulder high on the mountainside when he heard a child's sniffles coming from a snow covered brush thicket. Finding the **u-sdi a-gi-lv**, he carried her back home.

The neighbors gathered full of questions about the **u-sdi a-gi-lv** surviving the night in the bitter cold and remaining dry in the heavy snow. Why wasn't she hungry, and how did she climb so high up the mountain?

The **u-sdi a-gi-lv** gave only one answer, "I went with the Little People, **Yûñ´wi Tsunsdi´**."

When Cherokee parents ask children to come in from play before dark, they should listen closely and carefully obey. The Little People go about freely at night so they will not be seen. If they see a child out after dark, when they are supposed to be inside, the Little People will play tricks on them.

If children find themselves out after dark and need help in finding their way, they can tell the unseen Little People who they are and where they are going, and they will not play tricks but will watch over them and see that they get there safely.

The same thing is true of adults out at night doing things they are not supposed to do. But the tricks they play on adults are stronger.

The Cherokee, **Tsa-la-gi**, have always been gatherers from the ever-providing mountains. It was the women who knew when to look and where to go. On this day, the wild blueberries, **ka-wa-yv**, were ripe and a group of girls trailed through the rugged mountains carrying their baskets to their favorite blueberry, **ka-wa-yv** patch.

Laughter, jesting and teasing dominated the girl-talk and caused the purpose to be less like work. They arrived to find that the **ka-wa-yv** were plentiful and kept them busy for a while.

One by one as baskets got full they met again for the walk back. One of the girls had not yet appeared, and after waiting an alarming length of time they set out to hunt for her, calling her name but not receiving an answer. They knew that she would not wander very far because it was understood by all that they were to always stay close together. It seemed that she had just disappeared. Two of the girls hurried home to report what had happened, and the men came quickly to start the search.

Thick clouds, **u-lo-gi-lv**, hid the sun, **nv-dv**, and a promise of rain, **a-ga-sga**, hurried them to the **ka-wa-yv** patch where they found the bewildered girls and began their search.

"Are you looking for me?" the missing girl's voice startled everyone.

"Where have you been?" They all seemed to ask at once.

"Nowhere!" she answered. "I've been here picking berries."

They exchanged confused looks confirming the impossibility of the situation, because she would have heard them calling as they searched.

One man, looking at her closely, knew that she had been with the Little People, **Yûñ´wi Tsunsdi´**, and knowing that she should not talk about it, lest there be difficult circumstances to contend with, motioned the others to silence and guided everyone home.

Stop it!" screamed a young boy, **a-tsu-tsa**, after receiving a hard throw of a baseball, **a-l(a)-sga-ti**, from his older brother, **a-gi-do**. Although near tears, he didn't want his **a-gi-do**, to know how bad it hurt.

His **a-gi-do** was hot from the mid-summer day and very bored. Finding his own entertainment, he threw the **a-l(a)-sga-ti** again, just as hard and past his younger brother into the woods. He then turned away and joined the shade of a nearby tree.

Frustration finally released tears from the young **a-tsu-tsa** as he ran after the **a-l(a)-sga-ti**, more to hide than to bring it back.

"It's over here!" a strange voice summoned. The young **a-tsu-tsa** followed.

"Come this way!" Again, he sought the **a-l(a)-sga-ti** in the direction of the voice, going first one way then another as the voice drew him deeper and deeper into the woods until he realized that he was lost.

The young **a-tsu-tsa** looked around the unfamiliar surroundings, knowing that the light was fading, but not knowing the way home. He panicked and threw himself on the ground in great tears, sobbing until he drifted off to sleep.

He awoke early the next day with someone shaking his shoulders. "Dad?" he asked trying to see through his swollen eyes.

"It's time to go home," his dad answered, picking him up from the ground and into his arms.

After feeling secure once again with his dad, he admitted timidly that he had gotten lost.

"Sometimes the Little People, **Yûñ´wi Tsunsdi´**, lead you away," his dad said, trying to take the blame from his son.

"Can they talk to you?" the **a-tsu-tsa** asked, raising his head and looking straight into his dad's face.

"Yes, son, they can. Did you hear them?"

He told his dad all that had happened, and his dad held him close all the way home. When they returned, the **a-l(a)-sga-ti** was at its usual place, but no one in the family had found it or put it there.   95

A family was leisurely gathered around the kitchen table after dinner, talking and drinking coffee. Their youngest child, a little girl, **u-sdi a-ge-yu-tsa** came in from playing, reached up on the table until her fingers found the cornbread, **se-lu-ga-du**, took a piece and rushed back outside. Soon she came back in for more. The mother asked, teasingly, "Aren't you eatin' a lot of **se-lu-ga-du**." With no answer, she again rushed back outside.

The next day, after dinner and during coffee, the **u-sdi a-ge-yu-tsa** came several times again for **se-lu-ga-du**. "What are you doing? You can't be hungry!" her mother exclaimed.

"I'm not, but the girl outside is hungry," the **u-sdi a-ge-yu-tsa** responded as she hurried back out again.

The next day, the same routine took place again. The family assumed that the **u-sdi a-ge-yu-tsa** was playing "pretend" and had an imaginary friend outside. As she returned for more, her mother grabbed her to her lap and held her laughing, "Where has all the **se-lu-ga-du** gone?" she asked, rubbing her daughter's tummy, trying to get her to laugh.

But her daughter was frustrated and said, "The girl outside wants it. She comes after we eat and always wants **se-lu-ga-du**." The mother would not let her daughter down from her lap, although she was squirming to go.

"Who is the girl outside? What does she look like?" she asked her daughter in a more serious tone.

The daughter described the mystery girl until her mother was satisfied, thinking that now she could go back out again. "Can I meet her?" the mother asked.

"Yes, she's in the backyard," the **u-sdi a-ge-yu-tsa** said and led her mother outside.

Anxiously, the rest of the family waited until they returned. Bursting through the door a bit irritated the **u-sdi a-ge-yu-tsa** stated, "The girl outside has gone home now, but I left her **se-lu-ga-du** where she eats."

The mother did not allow further discussion on the matter until her daughter was grown. The daughter's memory of the "girl outside" has faded and gone, but her family, who still lives in Birdtown, remembers well.

Across the road from a house on Soco Mountain, there is a very large, leaning tree. Occassionally, the people living in the house have watched two "kids" run up the steep tree, turn and walk back down. Children in the area could never climb a tree so steep. Sometimes the "kids" would motion for the neighborhood children to come and join them. Being tempted they would ask their parents and hear, "Go ahead, if you want to leave and never come back." Usually, they were no longer tempted.

The same family has a laurel thicket below their house, and many times they have heard sounds of laughter and playing coming from there. The children sometimes want to investigate but are warned that the "brownies" play there and they are not children like themselves. Caution is instilled to "leave them alone so the 'brownies' will not bother you."

> **Note**: The parent's terms "kids" and "brownies" in the above context were referring to the Little People. It has long been suffered by the Cherokee people that from time to time a child would be lost to the forest from a mother's watchful eye and never be seen again. It was commonly thought that the Little People might have taken them.

Warm winds and sunny days had brought along overdue melts of snow and the Oconaluftee river, **a-ma-ya**, was challenging its banks.

A group of daring boys were headed for a favorite place where a grapevine hung over the **a-ma-ya**. The vine had wrapped itself around the branches of a huge tree and was attached near the top.

Today the **a-ma-ya** ran fast and hard. They pulled the vine to a boulder where they launched into a wide swing, circling out over the **a-ma-ya** and back again. The treacherous **a-ma-ya** made it more daring and exciting. Everyone took their turn, showing their bravery.

The next day, the **a-ma-ya** was still running wild and so were the boys. Racing back to the vine, they arrived to find it gone. "That's impossible!" said one of the boys. "No one can climb that far up." He pointed to the place where the vine had been cut.

"Yes they can," said a voice from behind them. They turned to see that it was a man who lived nearby. He continued, "The Little People, **Yûñ´wi Tsunsdi´**, live here, and it looks like they were protecting you from your own foolishness."

Bright sunshine, **a-ga-li-ha**, washed down out of a blue sky, **sa-ko-na-ge ga-lo-lo**, sifting through the trees and spotting the path, **wa-ga-lo-hi-sdi**, a young man, **a-wi-na**, was following. It was a great day for just wandering through the woods alone as he had planned.

In the distance he saw children playing and heard their laughter. He quickened his steps to get a closer look. Suddenly he stopped, stunned. They were not children; they were Little People, **Yûñ´wi Tsunsdi´**. They moved on ahead of him jumping and darting around, climbing and bending saplings to launch themselves through the air. They played, and he followed. When he got close, they moved away. There were nine of them and soon they went around a bend and disappeared. Unable to find them again, the **a-wi-na** took a lower **wa-ga-lo-hi-sdi**

He had not gone far on the **wa-ga-lo-hi-sdi** when he was hit by a stick. He put his arms over his head. Sticks, leaves and debris fell from the **wa-ga-lo-hi-sdi** above. He ran, but it did not stop. He ran off the path winding one way and then another. It did not stop.

He yelled, "I did not come looking for you. We happened to be on the same **wa-ga-lo-hi-sdi**. Please stop!"

When he asked, they stopped.

Little People, **Yûñ´wi Tsunsdi´**, like to play around the waterfalls, **a-m(a)-ga-da-o-sga** that are all over the mountains. The Cherokee, **Tsa-la-gi**, children, **di-ni-yo-tli**, like to play there, also.

One mother, **e-tsi**, often took her **di-ni-yo-tli** to play in a shallow pool formed by the **a-m(a)-ga-da-o-sga**. The **di-ni-yo-tli** always loved it. The **e-tsi** used it as a way to get them clean.

One day while all this enjoyment was going on, rocks and sandy dirt came down on their heads. The **e-tsi** put them back into the water to wash it out of their hair. When they were once again clean, and she was drying them off, it happened again. Someone was throwing it on them. But no one was there.

The **e-tsi** repeated the process quickly and did not take time to dry them.

Leaving, they gave the, **Yûñ´wi Tsunsdi´** their privacy back, hoping that they would not play tricks on them on the way home.

102

CHEROKEE
WOMEN
and the
Yuñwi Tsunsdi'

A new mother, **e-tsi**, walked softly into her baby's bedroom to watch her sleep. It was almost time to feed her and she wanted to be beside the crib when her daughter, **a-qwe-tsi**, awoke. But she stopped, startled, when she saw a little woman no more than two feet tall peering into the crib. She was slender, with long black hair that fell over her shoulders. She wore a simple white dress that seemed to glow. The woman stepped away when the **e-tsi** saw her, and a moment later she had vanished.

A young woman, **a-ta**, who lived in the Painttown Community was in her yard putting wash, out to dry when she suddenly felt herself being watched. She looked all around but could see no one. So she decided to ignore the feeling.

The day, **i-ga**, was bright, **tsu-la-si-di**, and the breeze, **sdi-ga-no-la-v-sgv**, was gentle. She continued to hang clothes until she heard a sound. Not quite sure what it was, she strained to listen, to try and catch something on the edge of her hearing. She slowly turned around to see a little man sitting on the point of her roof, **ga-sa-na-l(i)**, his feet crossed, his back against the chimney. He was less than three feet tall.

For a few moments, they stared at each other, then he swung his feet around and disappeared over the other side of the **ga-sa-na-l(i)**. She hurried around the house, but did not see him again. She never found out why he was there.

105

In mid-summer, with more daylight to finish chores, the evening meal is often delayed. It was late when one woman, **a-ge-ya**, finished cleaning the kitchen, **a-da-sdi-ti**, and had just taken a sip of coffee, **ka-wi**, when she felt a tug on her apron, **a-tse sa-du-d(a)**. Her family, already enjoying their **ka-wi** , stopped their conversation and watched. Through the cat-hole of their log cabin, **a-da-ne-lv**, came a small arm, the size of a child's but looking more like that of an adult, and it grabbed the **a-tse sa-du-d(a)** tugging vigorously, almost pulling it through the hole in the wall. The **a-ge-ya** held on with both hands.

"Give me my **a-tse sa-du-d(a)**," she said as she pulled back. "It's mine!" She gave it one last hard yank.

Everyone told her that it was the Little People, **Yûñ´wi Tsunsdi´**.

"I know who it is," she replied, "but they are not getting my **a-tse sa-du-d(a)**."

In Piney Grove on Big Cove Road, a story is told about a woman, **a-ge-ya**, who was found dead with a gunshot wound in the back of her head. No one had robbed her and there were no suspects. They found a gun, **ga-lo-gwe**, beside her, recently fired, as if she had been shooting it out the window, **tso-la-ni**, at somebody. One neighbor's boy claimed he saw the Little People, **Yûñ´wi Tsunsdi´**, in her yard.

Everyone knew she did not like the **Yûñ´wi Tsunsdi´**, and she had shot at them before to scare them away. They later discovered that the bullet that killed her was her own and had ricocheted back into the house and hit her in the back of the head. The case has never been closed.

A young woman, **a-ta**, who had lived in the same house with her parents all her life was moving out on her own. It was both a sad and an exciting time.

During her last night at home, she and her parents had spent the time remembering many endearing events of her life with them.

"Did you hear that?" she asked her parents as she went to look out the window, **tso-la-ni**. "Listen."

The sound was getting louder and louder. Popping sounds, walking and talking sounds drifted in the **tso-la-ni** .

Her Father, **U-do-da**, smiled. "You know what that is," he said, and they all exchanged smiles of acknowledgment. Her Mother, **E-tsi**, reminded her that those Little People, **Yûñ´wi Tsunsdi´,** had been around since she was born, and even before that, when Grandfather, **E-du-du**, was growing up. They always took care of him and his family.

"I suppose they knew that this was your last night home," her **U-do-da** said. "Maybe it's their way of saying 'good-bye, **do-na-da-go-hv-i**.'"

The popping sounds approached the house, circled it and went back the way they came. She felt a little lonely and homesick when they all went to bed for the night.

For the next few weeks, the **a-ta** was busy moving, settling into her new place, having her friends, **o-ga-li-i**, over and sharing happy times. Then one night, she heard voices outside. Expecting **o-ga-li-i** to come by, she eagerly opened the door for them. But no one was there. The voices sounded clear and close by, so she stepped outside and looked around. Still, no one was there, so she went back inside.

Listening, she heard the familiar popping sounds mixed with the voices. She smiled and relaxed. The **Yûñ´wi Tsunsdi´** had followed her to her new home.

𝔄 glow of light came through the fog, **u-ko-ha-di**, over a mountain trail toward a young woman, **a-ta**, standing in the doorway of her home in Piney Grove. She was waiting for her dad to return. She wanted to be the first of her family to tell him about the strange sheep, **u-no-de-na**, they saw in the yard earlier that night.

This time, the glow of light was her dad's lantern. She ran to meet him and told him everything she could before entering the house.

They all had settled in when they heard the sound of their dogs barking, mixed with threatening growls. Her dad went to see who was there. He, too, witnessed the **u-no-de-na**, larger than usual and with a white glow. He succeeded in scaring it away but was very puzzled.

Later, the **u-no-de-na** returned. This time her dad met it with a gun and shot twice over its head, before it actually disappeared. Suddenly, he remembered how the Little People, **Yûñ´wi Tsunsdi´**, sometimes disguised themselves in unusual forms of animals.

Four days later a family member died. The family was not sure whether the **u-no-de-na** had come as a warning of the death or whether the death was a result of dad's shooting at it.

𝔍t was about the time refrigerators and freezers started showing up on the Cherokee, **Tsa-la-gi**, Boundaries. One spring, **go-ge-i**, a woman, **a-ge-ya,** bought a new freezer and extended her vegetable garden, **a-wi-sv-di**. Meanwhile, she gathered blackberries, **nu-ga-tli**, blueberries, **ka-wa-yv**, and strawberries, **a-ni**. She froze many things in her new freezer and canned goods for her cellar. She tended her **a-wi-sv-di** so well its yield kept her busy all summer, **go-gi**.

Soon, her freezer was full and her cellar shelves were overstocked. Later she gathered pears, **se-di i-yu-sdi**, and apples, **sv-ta**, and made jellies, **u-ga-na-sda ga-da-lv-dv-i**. She filled baskets with a variety of nuts but still she planned a three-day weekend to dig potatoes, **nu-na**, for her already bulging cellar.

When she returned home from the weekend, late in the day, she discovered that her freezer had malfunctioned and all of its contents were lost. Upon going to the cellar, much to her horror, she found all her jars of canned food knocked from the shelves and their spoiling contents mixed with the spilled goods from the many baskets. Everything was ruined and all of her gathering and hard work was in vain. She ran from the house in a panic.

Going to her uncle, who was a Medicine Man, **Di-da-nv-wi-sgi**, and wise about strange events, she told her horrible story and asked him what he thought had happened to all her food, **a-l(u)-sdi-di**.

He listened intently to her whole story before replying, "Your husband is no longer living and your children are grown, and you have only yourself to feed. Did you need all that **a-l(u)-sdi-di** for someone else?"

"No."

He grinned at her slim figure and asked, "Did you plan on getting real fat this winter?"

She dropped her shoulders impatiently and would not answer.

"Wait here, I'll be back in an hour," he assured her as he left his house and disappeared into the night.

Time passed slowly for her as she waited and waited. He returned in exactly one hour.

"What did you need all that **a-l(u)-sdi-di** for?" he asked, squinting his eyes at her and waiting silently for her to answer.

"I don't know," she finally answered. "It all started when I bought my freezer." She obviously didn't know herself, why she had stored so impulsively.

"The Little People, **Yûñ´wi Tsunsdi´**, did this for you," he told her. "Accumulating more than one's current requirement is detrimental to one's spirit."

The next year, again, she planted her extended **a-wi-sv-di**, gathered berries, **u-ta-nv-hi**, fruits, and nuts. She canned and filled her freezer and cellar with enough to take her through one winter, then traded for other things she needed and gave the rest away. Her **a-wi-sv-di** yielded more and more each year.

~~~

Now strange it was for two women, who enjoyed talking to each other over the telephone, **a-l(a)-si-l(a)-do-to-di**, when the connection would go bad every time their conversation turned to gossip. The phone would crackle and pop so bad that they would be unable to hear each other.

In discussions with their other women friends, they, too, had noticed the same type of bad connections from time to time. After investigation, neither the weather nor the **a-l(a)-si-l(a)-do-to-di** service had been a factor in disturbing the lines.

One day an elderly woman, known to practice "Indian Medicine", overheard these women complaining about the **a-l(a)-si-l(a)-do-to-di** static. "It happens just as I want to pass on certain information and at no other time," one woman complained.

"Gossip!" the elderly woman firmly stated.

The two women looked at each other, denying that their conversation was gossip.

"Remember clearly!" warned the elderly woman.

The two women would not look at each other this time nor did they speak.

The elderly woman continued, "The Little People, **Yûñ´wi Tsunsdi´**, often interfere with gossip. Sooner or later you will be faced with what you said. The **Yûñ´wi Tsunsdi´** try to protect you. If you can't keep from gossiping, you may get worse than **a-l(a)-si-l(a)-do-to-di** static, maybe an ear infection or a sore throat." She warned the women to pay attention to the warnings. "Gossip only makes fools out of the one doing it," she said.

Both remembered having sore throats and sore ears recently, but the elderly woman could not have known about that or about their tendency to gossip on the **a-l(a)-si-l(a)-do-to-di.**

The children, **di-ni-yo-tli**, were happily chasing each other around, squealing, with their dogs joining in and nipping at their heels. Their evidence of play was scattered everywhere about the yard.

Their mother was thinking how hard it was to keep her yard, from being messy as she picked up more and more items she thought were useless on her way to the garbage can.

She always had more garbage than anyone else. Lots more. The "garbage pick-up" people were to come by early the next morning, and today she wanted to get as much out and ready for them as she could.

The next morning she awoke to find her garbage again, scattered all over the yard. This was not the first time this had happened.
She remembering, hurriedly gathered it up to get it back in place for the "garbage pick-up" people.

As she was fussing about neighboring dogs, **di-ni-yo-tli**, or even the bears doing this to her she heard a voice say, "It's the Little People, **Yuñwi Tsunsdi'**, doing this to you."

The mother approached an old woman at the edge of her yard who had been watching her. "How do you know?" she asked rudely.

"It's their way," the old woman nodded her head knowingly. "They do this to the ones who are being wasteful." The old woman continued walking.

The mother was stunned as she watched the old woman travel on down the road. She suddenly wanted to call her back, but didn't know her name. She had never seen her before. And, she never saw her again.

From then on, the mother was careful with her accumulations of food, clothes, toys and household items. What she could not use any longer, she quickly gave to people who could. Her yard remained clean, her garbage was minimal, and her neighbors were appreciative.

Tsawa Si and Tsaga Si are two Little People brothers, who help the hunter.

There are many very small Little People, so small that some people call them fairies. They live in the forest and maintain balance between animal and hunter.

When the hunter respects the forest, has an honorable hunt, uses what he takes and takes no more than he needs, they will help him find game and see him safely home.

One must acknowledge them if he wants their help. If one is a dishonorable hunter, they can cause the game to be scarce, accidents to happen and illnesses to occur.

CHEROKEE MEN

and the

Yuñwi Tsunsdi'

If a man takes his relatives the animal, the bird, the fish, the insect, the trees and the plants for uses that are necessary in this life, he must realize that they are provided by Mother Earth and give thanks and honor them for their generosity. They, too, are allowed to take man and will return the honor.

Lynn King Lossiah

A neighbor, **na-v e-hi**, sat down on a fallen tree beside the road near an old log cabin. He waited for his **na-v e-hi**, an older man who lived there, who sometimes trapped with him. A fire crackled in the fireplace that could be seen through the open door of the cabin. He had already called to the old man. Obviously, he was not at home. The man waited.

The **na-v e-hi** often wondered how this older man could go away and leave his cabin open to stray dogs or cats, curious people, thieves or even wild animals. He remembered his cabin had never been bothered.

"Hey there!" The **na-v e-hi** heard a voice say as he saw the old man come from behind the cabin. "Been squirrel hunting. Come on in." So he followed the old man inside.

"Do you ever close up your cabin when you leave?" he asked.

"No, I don't need to," the older man replied, being aware of his neighbor's curiosity.

The **na-v e-hi** didn't ask anymore questions out of respect, but the old man sensed what he wanted to know and said, "My relatives are here when I am away."

The **na-v e-hi** knew that he didn't have any relatives and that he had lived in this cabin alone since he was a boy. The old man grinned as he saw the puzzled look on his neighbor's face and began to laugh, "You can't see my relatives, they are invisible." He anxiously waited for his neighbor's reaction to what he had said, but he did not reply so he continued, "They protect the cabin; no people or animals can come in while I'm not here.

You didn't, did you?"

The **na-v e-hi** thought about it. He could have entered the open door, but somehow he had chosen to wait outside. "I suppose you're right," he answered, realizing what the old man was referring to.

This opened up a long talk about the Little People, **Yuñwi Tsunsdi'**, who were the old man's relatives he mentioned.

*O*ne winter, **go-la**, two men decided to go 'coon hunting. Their search for game led them deep into the ice encrusted forests of the mountains, but they had little luck. The snow slowly sifted down, and their breath hung in the air about them like a cloud. Time passed and it began to grow dark. They stopped for the night under a rock shelf, built a fire and sat down to a warm can of beans, when they had visitors.

A party of Indians, **a-ni-yv-wi-ya**, in fur cloaks and boots began to pass by near the rock shelf. One of the **a-ni-yv-wi-ya** broke off from the group and came over to them. His hair was long and dark and shimmered with snow crystals. The smile on his face was warm and inviting. "We are having a feast!" he said. "Would you like to join us?" The hunters, **ga-ni-ga-no-li-do-hi**, took one look at their cans of beans and accepted the invitation, falling in behind the band of fur-clad strangers.

Before long, they arrived in a large clearing ringed by bright torches. Other **a-ni-yv-wi-ya** had already arrived. Music and dancing filled the bare clearing. The night sky above was dark and clear and full of bright, shining stars. And in the center of the clearing stood long tables covered with fresh fruits and vegetables from a summertime garden. Everyone ate,laughed, and sang and danced long into the night.

The festivities drew to a close as dawn grew near and many began drifting back into the woods. Their host led the **ga-niga-no-li-do-hi** back to their campsite as it began to snow again. The **ga-ni-ga-no-li-do-hi** thanked their host for the feast. The Indian, **A-yv-wi-ya**, smiled again and said, "Never speak of your time among us. Seven days will be all the time left to you should you ever break your silence."

When the **ga-ni-ga-no-li-do-hi** returned to town, they were full of stories. Their story spread like wildfire. People speculated on who the Indian, **A-yv-wi-ya,** might have been. The two **ga-ni-ga-no-li-do-hi**, however, did not speculate long. Within a week they were both dead.They had been with the Littlle People, **Yuñwi Tsunsdi'**.

I have walked and walked these mountains and couldn't get a trace of a deer, turkey or anything to bring home to my family," a man was expressing his bad luck to a friend.

"You've always been a good hunter," his friend said as he placed a long string of trout on the man's cleaning table. "My son is coming soon with venison for you and the family. That should last a while."

As they cleaned the trout, his friend asked, "Tell me more about this bad luck."

The man began, "It all seemed to begin when I was fishing one day. I had caught only two fish, one which I kept and another so small that I threw it over into the bushes. I didn't have another bite the rest of the day. Tried again later with no luck all morning, then when I did finally hang one, the 'big one,' it got away."

"Yeah, that's not good luck," said his friend. About that time he spotted his son coming with the venison.

The man remembered, "One day I hunted in the mountains all day without any action at all. I was so disgusted that I started shooting at anything. I shot birds, tree limbs, small animals, anything that moved.

"Hit anything? You've always been a good shot."

"I don't know. I was just practicing and didn't plan to eat them anyway," he answered. "I remember another day I'd been hunting with no luck. On my way down the mountain, I fell down a steep slope and tumbled to the bottom. I lost my shoes in the fall and had to climb back up to looking for them. Funny thing, when I found them the shoestrings were tied together. Never did figure that one out."

"You don't have to tell me anymore, that was the Little People, **Yuñwi Tsunsdi'**," his friend whispered.

"The **Yuñwi Tsunsdi'**! Are you sure?"
the man questioned but listened.

"Yeah," the friend said. "It's not the first time. One other hunter, **ga-no-li-do-hi**, who had removed his shoes, saw them tying his shoestrings, but the **Yuñwi Tsunsdi'** disappeared when he came closer. It seems that the **Yuñwi Tsunsdi'** expect more respect for the forest. Your trash, wasteful ways with fish and shooting around the forest just for sport is probably unappreciated by them. The **Yuñwi Tsunsdi'** expect a little more out of fisherman, **a-tsa hv-sgi,** and **ga-no-li-do-hi** than they do of others in the forest.

121

Twelve men were out hoeing Mr. Crowe's large cornfield. The sun, **nv-dv**, ascended and the air shimmered as some worked shirtless in the heat, **u-ga-na-wi**. One man straightened up, rubbing his back. Wiping the sweat from his forehead while looking around. He saw a small figure sitting on a fence not seventy feet away. He called it to the attention of the workers nearby. Before they could spot him, the little person had vanished. He briefly looked around, put his hat back on and resumed his work, **di-ga-lo-wisda-n(a)-ti.**

A short time later, someone else cried out, "Hey, look up there!" Everyone turned to see a small man, not three feet tall, watching them **di-ga-lo-wisda-n(a)-ti.** They questioned whether it might be the same one spotted on the fence earlier.

A loud noise distracted them all and upon returning their sight to the small man, he was gone.

One of the workhands who had worked in Mr. Crowe's cornfield for a long time said that he had seen the Little People, **Yuñwi Tsunsdi',** there before, but that they never hurt anyone. It seemed that they were just curious about who was working in the field.

A young deer hunter, **ga-no-li-do-hi**, had been in the woods a long time. The threat of another snow lay heavily in the air. This year, winter had come fast, food was scarce, and his hunt had been unsuccessful. He had eaten the last of his pemmican long ago and was getting weak from hunger. Night was pressing in, and he knew he had to turn back.

In a ravine he discovered some red berries, **gi-ga-ge u-da-ta-nv-hi**. In his hunger he ate all he could find. After a short time, a sharp pain went through his stomach, then another. He doubled over, fell to the ground and soon lost consciousness.

At home his mother was watching for him. He had been gone too long and she knew that something was wrong. When she could wait no longer she went into the woods to look for him. In the dawn's light she spotted him. Frost covered his clothes, and he had curled up against the chill of the night wind. His breathing was irregular, and he was sweating with a fever. She tried to awaken him, but all he could say was, "**Gi-ga-ge U-da-ta-nv-hi**."

She pulled and tugged until she got him into a standing position and leaning him against her. Step by staggering step, they started out of the woods. She was taking him to the "Indian doctor", Medicine Man. By the time they arrived, the young **ga-no-li-do-hi** was feeling better and walking on his own. He told the Indian doctor about the **gi-ga-ge u-da-ta-nv-hi**.

"Those berries are very poisonous. You could have died," he told him with great concern. "There is nothing I can do, or even need to do. The Little People, **Yuñwi Tsunsdi'**, have already doctored you and their medicine is stronger than mine."

He advised the young **ga-no-li-do-hi** to go home and remain still until his energy had returned. "The **Yuñwi Tsunsdi'** have great respect for a good **ga-no-li-do-hi**," he said. "They kept you alive."

There was once a fisherman, **a-tsa hv-sgi**, who loved to fish in the early morning. Often, he'd leave home before sunrise, pulling his boat to a nearby lake. Before the first rays of morning glimmered on the water he had his line out.

But one morning the **a-tsa hv-sgi** had trouble starting his motor. He checked the gas. He checked the oil. He tried it again. The motor sputtered and went silent. He cleared the intakes and checked the spark plugs. The sun began to peek over the trees as he worked. He looked for leaks in the gas line and checked the blades for tangled fishing line. Nothing seemed wrong. Everything looked to be in tiptop shape, except for the fact that the motor wouldn't start. He didn't know what else to do. He tried the motor one last time and it roared to life. The **a-tsa hv-sgi** took off his hat and tried to rub the stress out of the back of his neck. Then he shrugged his shoulders and headed out to his favorite fishing spot.

He almost didn't see it in time. He rushed to cut the motor and drifted close. There, just below the surface of the water, drifted a mass of tangled branches and debris. It was hard to see in the daylight, so the **a-tsa hv-sgi** would have had no chance to see it in the dark. If he had gone out any earlier, he would have gotten tangled and sunk his boat. He reached his secret fishing spot and silently in the daybreak, he watched the now silver lake.

A fish thrashed the water in pursuit, or escape. The **a-tsa hv-sgi** thanked the Yuñwi Amia Yune, the water dwelling Little People, for protecting him from disaster.

Dark was closing in on a group of loggers, and they knew how dangerous the high mountains could be for them if they tried to come down in the dark.

"Hurry up, I can't control these horses, **so-gwi-li**," yelled the logger who drove the team.

"What's wrong with them?" one asked another as they watched the unruly animals.

"Turn them loose. They know their way home!" he yelled.

"Look," said the other as he released the **so-gwi-li**, pointing toward a light hovering near the ground, glowing in the approaching darkness and moving toward them. "That may be the problem!"

"Ahwe," one logger whispered. " The fire carriers," **Astil-dihye-gi**.

As the light came closer, a logger was walking toward it as if in a trance. When he got near it, the light flew away and disappeared. So did the loggers, but in the opposite direction.

CHEROKEE ELDERLY

and the
Yuñwi Tsunsdi'

At dawn, as at birth,
*   the way is clear.*
In mid-life
*   all goes adrift*
*   in the glare*
*   of the noon-day sun.*

Only in the evening of life
*   do we look back*
*   and wonder*
*   at where we have been,*
*   what we have learned*
*   and why.*

The elderly among the Cherokee like to stay in their own homes after their children grow up and move out on their own. Some are left to live alone when their spouses pass away. Their age often keeps them from working very much. They like to save their energy for visiting friends and relatives.

Sometimes, when elders live alone and have no one to watch their homes while they are sleeping or away. They have their own way of calling on the Little People for help. They leave small portions of food out for them from time to time as a way of saying, "Thank You."

Often, when the elder awakens or returns, the Little People let them know who had come by. If they didn't want the visitor there, they have been known to throw rocks, dirt, sticks or pine-cones at them until they went away. If the visitor resisted leaving, the tactics of the Little People would sometimes become more and more serious.

This service of protection by the Little People is often very comforting to elders with hearing loss and much appreciated when naps are being enjoyed.

There was a farmer, **di-ga-lo-ge-sgi**, who had little in the way of earthly possessions. The only things he owned of value were some gold coins given to him by his father when he was young. His sons knew about the coins and would often argue about who would get them when the **di-ga-lo-ge-sgi** passed away. It saddened the old man to see his sons against each other. He did not like the gold coins and wished to be rid of them.

One day, the **di-ga-lo-ge-sgi** left his house, walking through the woods to decide what to do with the gold coins. The air was cool and damp, and a robin called from the overhead branches. He followed the faint sighing of the wind down old and familiar paths which led beside rushing creeks and splotches of green moss.

Although enjoying his walk he walked a little too far into the woods, and, growing tired, he sat down near the entrance to a cave. He heard rustling in the underbrush near him and watched. He expected a squirrel or rabbit to come bustling into the clearing. Instead, two small people stepped into view. Their long hair was as dark as night and flowed over their shoulders like black silk. The farmer was startled at first, but deep inside his old heart he knew these were the Little People, **Yuñwi Tsunsdi'**.

The **Yuñwi Tsunsdi'** smiled and invited him into their cave for a meal. A cooking fire was burning warmly when they entered. Meat was roasting over the flames. The smell of food appealed to his appetite, and as they ate together one of them said, "You are a long way from home."

"Yes," the **di-ga-lo-ge-sgi** replied. "At least it seems so. I really don't know where I am."

"How did you find the cave?" another one asked.

"I was only wandering," said the **di-ga-lo-ge-sgi**. "I didn't set out to find it."

"I can tell that you are very sad," remarked yet another being curious.

"Yes," the **di-ga-lo-ge-sgi** agreed, and then told the **Yuñwi Tsunsdi'** about all the problems the gold coins were causing his family. He shared his confusion about what to do.

130

When he finished talking, the **Yuñwi Tsunsdi'** whispered to one another and then turned back to the **di-ga-lo-ge-sgi**. "If you wish," one of them said, "you may leave the gold coins with us and we will bury them here."

The **di-ga-lo-ge-sgi** accepted their offer and expressed how happy he was. Now his sons would have no reason to fight anymore.

He thanked the **Yuñwi Tsunsdi'** for their generosity, and they talked together around the fire until the **di-ga-lo-ge-sgi** fell asleep.

When he woke, he found himself at the edge of the woods by his house. His sons stood over him, relief on their faces. He had been missing for days and they had feared never seeing him again. They helped him into the house. He told them all he could remember. They cared for him all day until he was rested and recovered from his walk. Neither brother had any cross words for the other this time.

The **di-ga-lo-ge-sgi** told them to never go looking for the gold coins, ever. He told a strange story about gold sometimes carries a curse. If a man was infected by the curse he would go crazy for gold, always seeking it above anything else and would spend his life trying to get more and more. As he got more he would lose friends and family. And the gold would leave his hands as fast as he possesed it.

The brothers remembered what it had done to them and the family. "Never tell your children or anyone else about the coins," the **di-ga-lo-ge-sgi** made them promise. He said a silent "thank you", **wa-do**, to the **Yuñwi Tsunsdi'** again for bringing peace to his family.

The next morning the **di-ga-lo-ge-sgi** did not wake. His sons buried him in the family cemetery. Some say the story ended there, the brothers never thought about the gold coins again. Others say that the **di-ga-lo-ge-sgi** made a mistake in telling them where the coins were buried. According to them, the brothers found the cave and attempted to dig for the gold coins, but mysteriously, a landslide started that sealed the cave forever.

Lynn King Lossiah

A loud knocking at the door disturbed a Cherokee man from his warm fire on a snowy winter's night. Answering the door, he found no one there, and when he looked around a bit he was greeted by only the brisk, cold wind.

Later, with furrowed brow, he answered a second "knocking." Looking around he again found no one nor were there any footprints in the newly fallen snow he noticed.

Again, the "knocking" came. This time he picked up his shotgun and yelled to the offender, "If you don't tell me who you are, I'm letting go with both barrels."

A reply came through the door, "It's your neighbor from across the mountain. What makes you so mad?"

The man quickly opened the door and apologized to his friend, asking "Why did you knock and then leave?"

"I only knocked this one time," his friend answered, confused at the implication.

Over steaming coffee, beside the roaring fire, they reminded each other how the Little People would often knock before a visitor would arrive.

The squeaking rocking chair seem to be keeping time as the day dwindled, and a Cherokee woman waited on the porch of an elder she wanted to visit. She was enjoying her leisurely wait for him to return home when suddenly, a wood chip came out of nowhere and hit her on the knee. Soon, chips were flying everywhere. She looked to see who was throwing them, but there was no one there. As more chips came more and harder, she left the rocking chair, ran across the porch, down the steps and through the yard. Wood chips following her all the way.

The next day the woman contacted the elder to inquire about a convenient time to visit. He invited her over that afternoon and told her not to be concerned about the events of the previous day. "The Little People protect my house when I'm away," he said.

A man who had always refrained from seeking help from other people found himself in a predicament. He sought the aid of a friend, borrowed money and now circumstances prevented him from repaying the loan at the time agreed upon. He was an honorable man and deeply felt his obligation.

Early one morning he went into the woods and walked a long way, following Soco Creek. "**Kislahlah joosti kistalah**," he repeated, "Help me, Little People, help me."

Growing weary, he rested on a rock and was staring into the water. A leaf fell on his shoulder, and then another on his other shoulder. Several more leaves, **tsv-ga-lo-ga**, fell close around him. Upon close examination he found that they were chestnut **tsv-ga-lo-ga**. After looking around to assure himself that no chestnut trees were in the area and that the **tsv-ga-lo-ga** were not carried by the wind, he began to gather up each leaf. He had not seen a chestnut tree in quite a while. When he had gathered all the **tsv-ga-lo-ga**, one by one, he headed back down the mountain to his friends house from whom he had borrowed the money.

He knocked on the door and was invited inside. He explained his circumstances to his friend and placed the **tsv-ga-lo-ga** on the kitchen table.

"I didn't loan you **tsv-ga-lo-ga**," said his friend. The man nodded in understanding and left, leaving his friend puzzled over the gesture. In a few minutes he, too, left to continue his chores, giving the matter little more thought.

The day ended and, returning from his chores, the friend went back inside his house. There on the kitchen table was money where the **tsv-ga-lo-ga** had been. He counted the money and found it to be the exact amount the man had borrowed.

STRANGERS

and the
Yuñwi Tsunsdi'

A stranger in a land would walk quietly,
    observing the ways of the people,
    listening for places to apply usefulness,
Humbly asking the way.
It is not the way of strangers to expect,
    have opinions,
    share attitudes,
    and, especially, to instruct.

Many times the noises around a house, inside or outside, are caused by the Little People, **Yuñwi Tsunsdi'**, to scare strangers away. Sometimes the commotion is so great that the visitors never come back. The **Yuñwi Tsunsdi'** are curious when someone comes around that they do not know or do not like.

They were not friendly when unwelcomed relative, **di-da-tse-li-hi**, of an elderly woman came to her trailer to stay for a while. They didn't want the relative, **di-da-tse-li-hi**, to stay even for one night. They rocked the trailer on and off all night, and the **di-da-tse-li-hi** couldn't sleep.

The next evening, after the **di-da-tse-li-hi** had spent the day catching up on sleep, the elderly woman asked him to take out the trash. He was gone so long that she began to wonder, hopefully, if the **di-da-tse-li-hi** had gone somewhere else to stay.

Late that night, the **di-da-tse-li-hi** finally returned, and told of hearing voices and laughter on the way to the roadside trash cans and of going to investigate who it was and what they were doing. Following the sounds until he was lost and then spent a big part of the night wandering around in the dark trying to find the way until suddenly, there was the trailer.

She knew it was the **Yuñwi Tsunsdi'** who had rocked the trailer, but she refrained from telling. The **di-da-tse-li-hi** left the next day to find a different place to stay.

A young girl was visiting her Grandfather, **E-du-du**, at his house for a few days. After she had gone to bed the first night, she heard a rock, hit the side of the house, barely missing her bedroom window. She got out of bed to look outside. Then several rocks hit at once. She ran to her Grandfather's, **Un-n(i)-tse-li**, bedroom to tell him and to receive a little comfort, but he was asleep and she decided not to wake him. Returning to her bed, she pulled the covers up under her chin and listened quietly as the rocks kept hitting.

The next day, during breakfast, she asked her **E-du-du** if he had heard anything during the night. "Like what?" he asked.

"Oh, like someone throwing rocks against the house. Seems like someone was trying to break my bedroom window, all night long. I didn't sleep at all," she said sheepishly, trying to interpret his reaction to each statement.

After listening intently, he replied as he arose from the table. "I'll be right back."

"Where are you going?" she asked, startled at the thought of his leaving her alone.

"Don't worry. You'll be okay, and I'll be right back," he said as he smiled and left the house.

She watched him climb the trail behind the house and go out of sight up the side of the mountain. She watched for his return, her eyes rarely leaving the trail where she had last seen him. About mid-afternoon she finally saw him coming and hurriedly prepared his lunch. Though very anxious to hear where he had gone, she tried to appear relaxed and calm as he came in the door.

He smiled and patted his stomach. "Smells good," he said. "I'm hungry." As he began to eat he continued, "You won't be bothered by the rocks again. It was the Little People, **Yuñwi Tsunsdi'**. They look after me and this house. They mistook you for a stranger and were trying to scare you away. I explained that you were my granddaughter and would be visiting me a few days."

The granddaughter was not bothered again during her visit nor upon any subsequent visit to **Un-n(i)-tse-li** house.

There was once a stranger, **ka-lo-i**, who moved into a long vacated house on a mountainside. Although it was dust covered and had an un-kept yard, he liked the secluded location. The man thought it was a perfect house for spending time alone. He was a writer and needed only the sparrows and wind as companions.

On the first night of residency the sounds began. He had just sat down after a long day of unpacking. Stacks of boxes still towered around him in the living room and the kitchen and peeking out of hallways. BUMPTHUMP!

The **ka-lo-i** sat up in his chair. He thought he had heard a sound, sort of like someone knocking. He listened. "Nothing," he thought. It must have been a tree limb against the house. He listened a little longer, but those sounds never repeated. Instead, he began hearing voices.

The voices seemed to be coming from the front porch. "Ah! Visitors!" the **ka-lo-i** thought. He got up from his chair to weave his way among the boxes to open the door and greet them. The porch was empty. He stepped outside and glanced around the yard. No one was there. He went back inside and closed the door. BUMPTHUMP!

He decided to ignored it. Old houses are always creaking and endlessly settling. Nothing to be concerned about. He sat back down in his chair and tried to relax. He tried reading a book, but it did not hold his interest. Then the voices started again, louder this time. It sounded like they were marching around the house as they chattered away. One was singing, but the **ka-lo-i** could not make out the words.

Suddenly, it came to him. Kids! Kids playing pranks! He stumbled over the boxes trying to get to the door quickly enough to catch them. As he flung the door open the voices stopped. No one was there. Hoping to scare them away, he yelled, "I know you're out there!" He closed the door and the voices started again.

This went on for sometime, the man opening and closing the door, the voices stopping and starting, and the always empty yard. He even tried peering out windows and peeking out from closed curtains, but no luck. He never caught them. Finally he gave up, bolted the door, and went to bed.

That was when the "BUMPTHUMP, BUMPTHUMP, BUMPTHUMP" began in earnest. BUMPTHUMBUMPTHUMP-BUMPTHUMP! The **ka-lo-i**, groaned. BUMPTHUMP! He tossed and turned trying to keep a pillow over his ears. It was a long and BUMPTHUMP sleepless night. This continued for several days. Finally, in desperation, the **ka-lo-i** went to talk to his nearest neighbor.

"I wonder if you could help me?" the **ka-lo-i** asked. "I haven't slept since I moved into that house, and I've hardly worked on my writing." The whole story poured out about his dilemma.

The neighbor listened attentively with pursed lips and nodded his head until the **ka-lo-i** stopped talking. "It's the Little People, **Yuñwi Tsunsdi'**," he said.

"Yes," the man agreed, unknowingly. "I can't catch them. Do you know who these kids belong to and where they live?"

"Not kids," said the neighbor firmly. "The **Yuñwi Tsunsdi'**. Not the same."

"Not the same! How?" the man asked, not sure of what he was about to hear.

The neighbor explained the difference which left the **ka-lo-i** apprehensive, "I find that hard to believe," he said.

The people before you didn't find it hard to believe. They left when they learned that the house had been built long ago blocking one of the old trails of the **Yuñwi Tsunsdi'**. They found that to be inconsiderate.

The **ka-lo-i** listened further to the neighbor then thanked him and wandered home. That night he sat in his chair and listened to the BUMPTHUMPING. He listened to their singing and the rare genuine laughter that he had heard on few occasions. "It's not bad," he thought, "Not really, now that I listened to it." He had accepted it.

That night he put some food on the porch for them as the neighbor had advised. Then he went to bed and enjoyed a long, overdue, deep, undisturbed sleep.

OTHER RELATED BEINGS of the CHEROKEE

Nunne-hi :

The "immortals," "eternal ones," the "people who live everywhere, anywhere and forever," who go about invisible. Their power is so closely related to the Little People that one can hardly tell the difference. They more often appear to the Cherokee with the look and size of other Native Americans but can take on the look of the Little People at will. Unlike the Little People, however, they live underground. They sometimes appear as birds (mostly owls), animals, trees, fish, reptiles and even insects.

They are a race of spirit people that live in the mountain highlands and have many homes on high peaks and balds. They had large homes in Pilot Knob and under the old Nikwasi mound in North Carolina and under Blood Mountain at the heart of Nottely River in Georgia.

They are invisible except when they want to be seen. Like the Little People they enjoy music and dancing. Hunters in the mountains would often hear the dance songs and drum beating in some mysterious place, but when they tried to follow the sounds they would shift about, and hunters could never find them.

They are friendly people, too, and often brought lost wanderers to their homes under the mountains, cared for them until they were rested and then guided them back to their homes.

More than once when the Cherokees were hard pressed by the enemy, the Nunne-hi warriors have come out, as they did at old Nikwasi (the burial mound in Franklin, North Carolina) and saved them from defeat.

Soldiers who were in the Civil War asserted that they frequently saw smoke rising from the burial ground near Bryson City, North Carolina or from Kitu-hwa, an ancient settlement of the Cherokee where the Nunne-hi lived.

On the upper branch of Nottely River, running nearly due north from Blood Mountain, there is a hole, like a small well, in the ground from which comes an unexplained warm vapor that heats the air all around. It makes a nice warming place for hunters, but they don't stay very long, because the Nunnae-hi live there.

There are many more known homes of the Nunne-hi and many reports of association with them.

A tsil-dihye gi : The "fire-carrier".

Spirits that go about at night with a light. Not much is known about this spirit so it is avoided by the Cherokees. Considered dangerous and unfriendly, it always moves away when approached. Foreign people have called it the "will-of-the-wisp", a gaseous phenomena, ignis fatuus, which has been a thing of mystery and fear to others, in addition to the Cherokees. It moves away from them, too, when approached. The "fire-carrier" has been seen on occasion by the Cherokee loggers.

A tsi la-wa i : "Fire relative."

A peak spoken of as Rattlesnake Knob, along the Oconaluftee River in Cherokee in the Yellow Hill community. It receives its name from a tradition that a ball of fire can be seen to fly through the air from the direction of the highlands in Macon County and alight upon this mountain.

The Cherokee believe it to have been a Ulunsu'ti (rattlesnake) which the owner had kept in a hiding place upon the summit from which, after his death, came forth nightly to search for him. The light can often be seen until this day.

A nisga ya Tsunsdi : "Little Men."

Always represented as beneficent wonder-makers of great power.

These two sons of Kanati (first man), who are sometimes called "Thunder Boys," live in Usunhi-yi, above the sky vault. They must not be confused with the Yuñwi Tsunsdi' or Little People, who are also "thunderers," but who live on the earth and cause the short, sharp claps of thunder.

The "Little Men" have reproduced themselves by striking lightening very near a woman, giving birth to a human with the same characteristics as the Little People.

There is also the "Great Thunderer," the thunder of the whirlwind, tornado and hurricane, who seems to be identical with Kanati, himself.

The favorite honey locust tree, and the tree with thorns of the same species, is the home of the "Thunder-man," indicating to the Cherokee a great hidden connection between the pinnated leaves of the tree and the lightening.

A ni-hyuv tikwala ski: "Thunderers."

These beings are considered to be dangerous and powerful. Preside in the western skies beyond the celestial firmament.

Fairies :

These small beings live in hollow trees and on rocky cliffs as do the Little People. When confronted with uncertainty, they remain still and take on the look and smell of their environment, becoming hard to see. When in flight they are luminous, sometimes appearing as balls of light of different colors, but most often transparent white.

If an encounter is made with a fairy one should be completely quiet and give full attention. Also, people should never accept food from the fairies, because they would never be able to eat human food again nor return to their family.

Nugatsa-ni is a ridge below Yellow Hill said to be a resort of the fairies.

Two well known fairies are **Tsa-wa-si** and **Tsa-ga-si.** These two spirits are frequently named in the hunting prayers. All the woods and waters are peopled by hard to see fairy tribes, but these two small fairies, though mischievous enough themselves, often help the hunter who acknowledges them.

Tsawa-si or **Tsawa-si Usdi-ga** is a tiny fairy, very handsome, with long black hair to his feet, who lives in grassy patches on hillsides and has great power over game. To the hunter, he gives the skill to slip up on the deer through the long grass without being seen.

Tsaga-si is another very helpful spirit invoked by the hunter, but when someone trips and falls, it is usually known that it is he that has caused it. There are several other of these fairies with special names, all good-natured, but more or less tricky.

De tsata : A Boy who once ran away to the woods to avoid a scratching and has tried to keep himself invisible ever since. (A "scratching" is part of the Cherokee ceremony where scratches, usually to the back, are applied with an eagle claw, comb or other medicine object to bring blood.)

He is a handsome little fellow and spends his whole time hunting birds with the blow-gun, and bow and arrow. When a flock of birds flies up suddenly as if frightened, it is because De-tsata is chasing them. He is mischievous and sometimes hides an arrow from the bird hunter who may have shot it into a perfectly clear place, but looks without finding it. Then the hunter may say, "De-tsata, you have my arrow, and if you don't give it back, I'll scratch you." When the hunter looks again, the arrow will be there.

He has a great many children who are like him and who have the same name.

Dunwi Tsunsdi of the **Yuñwi Tsunsdi'** : The little people of the Little People are fairy like, their stature is no taller than the knee of the Little People. They often glow. They are powerful guides of the Little People and the medicine men of the mountains.

Yunwi Ama yine hi : "Water dwellers" who live in the water and who, when they are acknowledged, help the fishermen.

The spirit of the water often helped the Cherokee in illnesses of both body and mind. By "going-to-the-water" during **u-la-go-hv-sd**i (when leaves were on the water in autumn), the people were given protection from illness for the coming year.

The spirit of the water would be included during ceremonies such as preparations for ball games, battles, ani (sweat house) and when food was scarce.

Published by
CHEROKEE PUBLICATIONS

Preserving Cherokee Culture
Since 1956

Native Owned and Operated

**Cherokee Publications
P.O. Box 430
Cherokee, NC 28719**

Visit us at our online store

www.cherokeepublications.net

Call
1-800-948-3161
to request a FREE catalog

A retail and wholesale distributor of over 500 Cherokee and
Native American items.

To purchase original art, limited edition prints, and traditional Cherokee crafts from Lynn and Ernie visit their collection at

www.cherokeecollection.com

For commissioned artwork or to ask Lynn or Ernie to visit your shop, bookstore, museum, or school for book signings or cultural exchange, email Lynn at

cherokeecollections@verizon.net

Lynn is an art teacher, an award winning professional painter in oils, an illustrator and writer

Ernie, also an artist, a woodcarver, stonecarver and a traditional cedar flutemaker.

Lynn King Lossiah and her husband Ernie Lossiah reside in Cherokee, North Carolina. On the boundary of Eastern Band of the Cherokee Indians.

CHEROKEE SYLLABARY

D a	R e	T i	Ꮂ o	Ꮕ u	i v
Ꮝ ga Ꮕ ka	Ꮆ ge	Ꮿ gi	A go	J gu	E gv
Ꮧ ha	Ꮅ he	Ꮂ hi	F ho	Ꮆ hu	Ꮂ hv
W la	Ꮝ le	Ꮅ li	Ꮆ lo	M lu	Ꮏ lv
Ꮝ ma	Ꮍ me	H mi	Ꮝ mo	Ꮍ mu	
Ꮝ na Ꮝ hna	Ꮕ ne	Ꮒ ni	Z no	Ꮕ nu	Ꮕ nv
Ꮖ qua	Ꮝ que	Ꮖ qui	V quo	Ꮝ quu	Ꮝ quv
Ꮜ sa Ꮝ s	Ꮝ se	Ꮖ si	Ꮝ so	Ꮝ su	R sv
Ꮮ da W ta	Ꮝ de Ꮝ te	Ꮧ di Ꮝ ti	V do	S du	Ꮝ dv
Ꮝ dla Ꮝ tla	L tle	C tli	Ꮝ tlo	Ꮝ tlu	P tlv
Ꮯ tsa	Ꮩ tse	Ꮒ tsi	K tso	J tsu	C tsv
G wa	Ꮝ we	Ꮻ wi	Ꮝ wo	Ꮝ wu	6 wv
Ꮝ ya	Ꮝ ye	Ꮝ yi	Ꮝ yo	Ꮝ yu	B yv

Sounds Represented by Vowels

a, as a in father, or short as a in rival
e, as a in hate, or short as e in met
i, as i in pique, or short as i in pit
o, as aw in law, or short as o in not
u, as oo in fool, or short as u in pull
v, as u in but, nasalized

Consonant Sounds

g nearly as in English, but approaching to k. d nearly as in English but approaching to t. h,k,l,m,n,q,s,t,w,y as in English.